YOUR MARRIAGE...
HEAVEN OR HELL ON EARTH?

HOW TO HAVE A SWEET AND WHOLESOME MARRIAGE THAT MAKES YOU FEEL LIKE YOU ARE IN HEAVEN ON EARTH.

DR. TADIUS MAWOKO
(BBS; MBS; D. Min; Grad. Cert. Ed. Studies; MoC)

FOREWORD

I have known Dr. Tadius Mawoko and his wife Gwen as friends for over thirty-two years. For twenty-eight of those years, we have been fellow ministers of the gospel. Both Pastors Tad and Gwen have long been counselling and coaching couples, teaching at conferences and on TV, holding Couples' Seminars and releasing podcasts on marriage. With this in mind, it is no surprise that Dr. Tad's second book would be on marriage. This book, "Your Marriage...Heaven or Hell on Earth?" is well written, with hard truths about marriage, delivered with ample doses of humor. I highly recommend this book as a great reading, with honest, practical teachings which some, I believe, are from the very lives of Pastors Tad and Gwen, whose solid marriage has been exemplary and an inspiration to many. I believe anyone who will read this book will not only enjoy it thoroughly but will gain marriage-enhancing knowledge. Have your own heaven on earth marriage!

Apostle Dr. Stephen (Steve) Simukai. (D. Min).
Deputy Secretary General- ZAOGA- Forward in Faith Ministries Intl.

YOUR MARRIAGE… HEAVEN OR HELL ON EARTH?

TESTIMONIALS

I have known Dr. Tad and Dr. Gwen for almost thirty years now and I can testify boldly that the contents of this book are so practical in their marriage, and I have personally observed these principles in their own marriage. I like how they have made themselves vulnerable, exposing their own personal and intimate experiences in order to help the world's couples. The way Dr. Gwen used to compare her husband with her dad is very common among many couples and can be frustrating unless resolved. Dr. Tad's treatise on the five levels of communication and communication killers is on point and outstanding. My favorite is "real marriage is not for the selfish" where Dr. Tad shares on how we should minister to one another as couples. So profound. Read on and get your marriage transformed!

>**Evangelist George Rwizi**
>*BSc. Civil Engineering Honors (UZ), MSc in Cyber security (University of West Virginia), BA in Theology (New Life College), Diploma in Biblical Studies (AMFCC), Certified Cyber security Professional, Certified Ethical Hacker*

This is a book unlike many other marriage books. Dr Mawoko, from his very extensive experience and educational background, addresses today's social and cultural challenges in a marriage. Because of its relevance, it's a "must read"!

>**Alta Hatcher**
>*Doctoral Degree in Pastoral Psychology Integrity Seminary; Retired: Director of Advanced Leadership and Pastoral School /*

YOUR MARRIAGE... HEAVEN OR HELL ON EARTH?

> *Christ for the Nation's Institute; Retired: Member of American Association of Christian Counseling; Elder at New Hope Chapel Norwell, Ma.*

Dr. Tadius explores the biblical basis of a Christ-centred marriage thoroughly and clearly, using biblical background to demonstrate the basis of a Christ-centred union. Dr. Tadius uses the tools we have through Christ's life manual to enjoy and not endure marriage. Navigating the Christian marital landscape is a fundamental exercise we all must experience to enjoy the God-given benefits of marriage - love, joy, friendship, intimacy, and children. Every married couple, regardless of their stage in marriage, will find valuable insights to apply to their own relationships. The book offers a comprehensive discussion on love, intimacy, friendship, troubleshooting, handling the extended family, friends and community in a committed Christ-centred union using biblical principles and exposure. Dr. Tadius provides biblical tools for establishing our marital union, exploring, troubleshooting, and enjoying the journey, just as Christ did with the church. This is a commendable read and marital guide that I strongly recommend to every married couple (and to those planning a Christ-centered marital union). The book's engaging narrative and insightful content kept me captivated from start to finish.

> **Clifton Washaya**
> *MBChB, MMed (Surgeon), FCS (ECSA), FCS (SA), FRACS, FAMLC; Specialist Surgeon*

I would like to share with you something that has made a profound impact on my understanding of relationships lately. I recently finished reading YOUR MARRIAGE... HEAVEN OR HELL ON EARTH? and I simply couldn't put it down, and this is why I highly recommend it's a MUST-READ for anyone. The author offers incredibly insightful perspectives on the intricacies of marriage, shedding light on common challenges and providing practical explanations. This is for couples at any stage of their relationship. The practical advice, both biblical and research based strategies, as well as the author's inspiring stories will help you navigate the challenges of marriage and build a strong foundation for a lasting relationship. One of the key takeaways for me is in Chapter 4 on communication and the levels. Learning how to express needs, listen actively, and resolve conflicts constructively has made a significant difference in my own relationship which I have been in for 35 years now. Whether you're newlyweds or have been married for decades, there's something valuable to gain from this book. It's filled with practical tools and exercises that can help enrich any marriage, no matter the stage, there are tools for growth in this book. Overall, I truly believe that reading this book, YOUR MARRIAGE...HEAVEN OR HELL ON EARTH? can be transformative for anyone seeking to deepen their connection with their spouse and build a strong, long-lasting relationship. I highly recommend giving it a read. I'm confident you'll find it as enlightening as I did.

Melody Magengezha
President of Africa Women Summit – Australia; Host of Mbuya vaRaphy Talkshow; CEO Rising Serenity Coaching & Therapy Services; Founder of Mbuya vaRaphy Academy & Foundation Zimbabwe; Bachelor of Nursing – UNITEC New Zealand (NZ); Post Grad.Cert in Mental health – The University of Auckland; Diploma in Business studies and Pedagogics – Chinhoyi

University of Technology; Certificate in Dialectical Behavioural Therapy – DBT NZ;
Certificate in Relationship & Health and Wellness Coaching

Published in Australia by REVIVE MEDIA
Postal: P O Box 1361 Fitzroy North, Victoria 3068, Australia
Tel: +61 412 938 592/ +61 431 166 093
Email: tad@tadandgwen.com
Website: www.tadandgwen.com

First published in Australia 2024
Copyright ©Tadius Mawoko 2024

All rights reserved. No part of this publication may be reproduced, stored in a retrieval system, or transmitted in any form or by any means without the prior written permission of the publisher, nor be otherwise circulated in any form of binding or cover other than that in which it is published and without a similar condition being imposed on the subsequent purchaser.

Scriptures quoted are taken from the NKJV (New King James Version) © 1982 by Thomas Nelson, Inc. Used by permission. All rights reserved.

National Library of Australia Cataloguing Publication entry

A catalogue record for this work is available from the National Library of Australia

ISBN: # 978-0-6450145-5-6 (PAPERBACK)
ISBN: # 978-0-6450145-6-3 (EPUB)
ISBN: # 978-0-6450145-7-0 (AUDIO)

YOUR MARRIAGE... HEAVEN OR HELL ON EARTH?

Cover design by Takudzwa T.K. Nyamvura

Edited by Pamela Rutsito

Typesetting and Layout by Loraine Mubare (Loraine Print Designs)

Printed by REVIVE MEDIA

REVIVE
MEDIA

Disclaimer
All care has been taken in the preparation of the information herein, but no responsibility can be accepted by the publisher or author for any damages resulting for the misinterpretation of this work. All contact details given in the book were current at the time of publication but are subject to change.

The advice given in this book is based on the experience of the individuals. Professionals should be consulted for individual problems. The author and publisher shall not be responsible for any person with regard to any loss or damage caused directly or indirectly by the information in this book.

DR. TADIUS MAWOKO

DEDICATION

This book is affectionately dedicated to my wonderful wife Gwen who at the time of writing has been married to me for thirty-five years ... and these have been the best years of my life. She is my lover, best friend, intercessor, and constant prayer partner.

Gwen baby, doing life with you has been awesome. With God's grace let's keep this thing going - forever - till death do us apart!

My three children Bethel Tinashe, Bethany Ropafadzo, Belinda "Bells" Anenyasha and my "son-in-love" Ebenezer, all of whom I pray for every day, that among other things, God may bless them with sweet marriages like ours. I love you guys to the moon and back! My first grandchild Asaph Reagan...may God do wonders through your life!

To my future daughter-in-love (Bethel's future wife) and future son-in-love (Bells' future husband) - may marriage for you all, my children, be heaven on earth.

To all ministers who strive to teach on and counsel marriages and lead by example every day... may God reward you now and in eternity.

To all the couples whom we have counseled, and you recommitted to each other, cancelled divorce proceedings and renewed your vows - you know yourselves... here it is to you!

To all the couples who believe marriage is worth fighting for – may God stand with you!

ACKNOWLEDGEMENTS

To my spiritual parents, mentors, and counselors – the late Apostle Dr. Ezekiel H. and Apostle Dr. Eunor Guti - you were there for us from the very early days with your recorded teachings and then face to face teachings. You are our champions, and your teachings and books are a treasure to us. Thank you for not living double lives, but leading by example in all you did. Gwen and I are forever indebted to you, and we love you dearly.

Drs. Steve and LaVerne Simango - Simukai, Pastors George and Rudo "Love" River, Apostle Dr. Joseph Joe and Rev. Nyasha Guti, Apostle Dr. Pat M. Schatzline and the late Prophetess Deb, we as a couple acknowledge your friendship and support.

To all Forward in Faith pastors the world over; we are blessed to be a part of this army of young Ezekiels and young Eunors.

We also acknowledge all ministers who have opened their churches, couples' ministries and conferences for Gwen and I to do what we love best - minister and build marriages to be used by God in the Kingdom - thank you!

Acknowledgment also goes to all our several friends in the ministry. Lastly but not least, to my mother Mrs. Evejoice Sekai Mawoko who went home to glory in August 2017. Your labor of love, discipline, and dedicated support for me was not in vain.

YOUR MARRIAGE... HEAVEN OR HELL ON EARTH?

Lastly but not least, to Tariro Hove, my spiritual son who converted this manuscript from handwritten to Word. Thank you for your hard work.

TABLE OF CONTENTS

INTRODUCTION...

CHAPTER 1	Marriage is meant to be enjoyed as God intended	13
CHAPTER 2	Devotion and surrender to God	16
CHAPTER 3	The early years in marriage	20
CHAPTER 4	Communication in marriage	25
CHAPTER 5	Sex... Let's talk about it	42
CHAPTER 6	Money – Tithes, giving and saving	51
CHAPTER 7	Dealing with in-laws	55
CHAPTER 8	Other problems in marriage	65
CHAPTER 9	Grooming and ministering to each other	68
CHAPTER 10	Investing into your marriage	76
CHAPTER 11	Advice to men	80
CHAPTER 12	Advice to women	86
CHAPTER 13	Temperaments, Personalities and Character	95
CHAPTER 14	Birds of a feather... Choosing friends as a couple	102
CHAPTER 15	Fruitfulness as a couple	105
CHAPTER 16	Influencing and helping others	108
CHAPTER 17	Dealing with children	111
CHAPTER 18	Bodily exercise profits	117
CHAPTER 19	Keep boundaries	120
CHAPTER 20	The ugly truth about divorce	123
CHAPTER 21	Importance of a counselor	126
CHAPTER 22	Conflict resolution	130
CHAPTER 23	Renew and refresh your marriage	133
CHAPTER 24	Message to veterans	136
CONCLUSION		

YOUR MARRIAGE… HEAVEN OR HELL ON EARTH?

INTRODUCTION

Someone has said that marriage is the closest thing to heaven or hell that you can experience here on earth. So, for couples, marriages can be a foretaste of heaven here on earth, or hell here on earth. It is therefore up to the couple whether they want to live in a little heaven on earth or hell here on earth. Marriage is work, hard but rewarding and fulfilling work. It's never automatic, therefore each couple must decide. To have hell on earth is easy – simply do nothing and Satan, the opposer of marriage (and opposer of all things good and godly) will do the rest. He will wreck your marriage beyond repair and lead you to divorce and emotional, physical, and financial mess. Children become vulnerable to every wile of the devil like drugs, alcohol, depression, and all sorts of crime. The divorced parent normally goes through an almost unending time of pain, depression, shame, guilt, sense of failure and hopelessness God intervenes. Apostle Dr. Ezekiel Guti said it's like one losing an arm or a leg.

On the other hand, "Heaven on Earth" does not come easy either. God has promised us good things in His word, including wonderful, sweet marriages. But they do not just happen. A good marriage is a result of hard work and prayer, from dating till the end. Marriage is hard work and it's not for the faint hearted either. A sweet marriage is worked for, but with assurance that you will win because the battle is rigged in your favor. Sweet marriages that represent Christ and the Church relationships are the design and goal of God. Therefore, God will help us in our relationships to reach these God ordained destinies of marriage in our lives. God is always on our side, but you and I must do our part.

YOUR MARRIAGE... HEAVEN OR HELL ON EARTH?

Let me put it this way: from Genesis 12 vs 1, God Almighty calls out Abraham (then called Abram) from Haram – "to the land I will show you". You will realize that from Abraham, Isaac, Jacob, the Twelve Patriarchs, and during the era of Joseph in Egypt, God continued to confirm His promise of a land filled with milk and honey. Joseph believed this so much that he made the Israelites promise that when they leave Egypt, the land of bondage, they must carry his dead body with them to the promised land. So, when deliverance came, the Jews left Egypt for the promised land with Joseph's corpse. Some reference scriptures come from: Genesis 50 vs 24, Exodus 13 vs 19 and Hebrews 11 vs 22.

Now here is the point: with all these promises that were sure, God led them through deserts and inhospitable lands to achieve this goal. The land of Canaan with its milk and honey was not handed over to Israel on a silver platter. Though it was their destiny, though it had been promised to them from Abraham's time and confirmed over and over, they did not waltz into it. THEY HAD TO FIGHT! That's my point exactly! Israel fought the Ammonites, the Amalekites, the Moabites, the Edomites, the Jebusites, the Canaanites and as one preacher said, "all the other 'ites'!" They had to fight for their God-given land.

My sister and my brother – fight for your marriage! Your Canaan in marriage is there! Your land of milk and honey is there – but you need to fight all these 'ites' to possess this land of joy, love, understanding, peace, trust, fidelity, happiness, amazing sexual satisfaction, great communication and prosperity. Such a marriage is possible, and you deserve it. It is your God-given portion. It's what God, the author of marriage designed for you. Go for it! Go for it you precious couple – go! The enemy will fight you, but all the odds are in your favor because God Almighty, Creator of heaven and earth,

Creator of the universe and Creator of marriages is on your side. He created and ordained marriage for us whom He created in His own image. So yeah – you surely can have a little heaven on earth! I dare you to go for it. You will enjoy the results of this effort for your whole lifetime.

#RiggedInYourFavor

CHAPTER 01

MARRIAGE – MEANT TO BE ENJOYED AS GOD INTENDED

Marriage was created by God. Just like all things created by our heavenly father, marriage is good and must bring joy and fulfilment to mankind. In all things that God created, the Bible says, *"...and it was good."* Genesis 1 v 25,31(a). In like manner, marriage is good, in fact it is very good. As said earlier, marriage is supposed to bring happiness, joy, emotional and sexual well-being but that is not always the case. The enemy of God, Satan, who is automatically our enemy has played havoc with our marriages and caused pain and unbearable suffering, bitterness and even death either by spousal killings or suicide. It was never meant to be this way.

Marriage, according to the pure plan of God, was meant to be a gift to mankind. And God only gives good gifts (James 1 vs 17). The devil has long declared war on marriage through rampant divorce and lately, all over the world through same sex "marriage" activists who are demanding that marriage be redefined. But the Author Himself has intended it to be a certain way. Of late, the devil has thrown even the kitchen sink at marriage because marriage is so dear to God's heart. God's definition and intention of marriage has always been holy, pure, happy, joyful, spiritual, sexual, and fulfilling. Why has the devil thrown even the kitchen sink at marriage?

To answer the above question, we need to go slightly deeper into the meaning and purpose of marriage. To understand this, we must ask another question – What is marriage?

The biblical meaning and connotation of marriage is:
1. Union of a man and woman in holy matrimony, that is, the union of two members of the opposite sex in spirit, body, and soul. Genesis 2 vs 24 states *"... and they shall become one flesh"*.
2. A union in their goals, dreams, and aspirations.
3. A surrender of self, and unconditional acceptance of a spouse (of opposite sex) into your life.
4. A covenant between man and a woman to cleave to each other, cherish each other in all circumstances whether good or bad.
5. A covenant between a man and a woman, to forsake all others and only to have and hold onto their partner.
6. To exemplify, all by God's grace, the union between Christ and His church (Ephesians 5 vs 22-23). Let's take special note of the verses 31 and 32 of Ephesians 5 – *"For this reason, a man shall leave his father and mother and be joined to his wife and the two shall become one flesh. This is a great mystery, but I speak concerning Christ and the Church."*

When we consider the last point above, we come to realize that the greatest purpose of marriage was and is to portray to the world the relationship between Christ and his Church. Christ is the groom (husband); and the church is the bride (wife). Christ is coming back to take his bride, the church without blemish according to Ephesians 5 vs 27. It is obvious now why the devil wants to distort and destroy marriages. Marriage as God intended it, is a powerful picture of Christ and His Church and a great tool for evangelism. My wife and I have been privileged by God with the grace of winning people to Christ as they simply observe our marriage – the way we relate. One such, has become a pastor in our church organization.

Every marriage must be an evangelism tool in the hands of Master Jesus. But if the marriage is broken and full of spite, the master cannot use it until it is restored. Your marriage, my brother and sister, is meant to be an awesome tool in the hands of God. But how can it be, if the unbeliever cannot find anything to emulate in your marriage? This is why if you both purpose to fight for your marriage, you will win because God who is the author of marriage has a purpose for it. Fight for your marriage. Even when things look bleak, like David before Goliath, say – "is there not a cause!"

Now we clearly see that marriage is surely intended to be enjoyed and not endured. God's gifts are good. Let us also remember that part of God's purpose for marriage is to bring godly seed into the world. It is important to note that the intention of God is to bring children into the world through married couples. This does not by any means render children born out of wedlock to be out of God's plan – no! He always makes all things beautiful in the end. Each child is born with a God-given purpose and destiny, whether born in or out of wedlock. However, the perfect will of God is to have children born within the bounds of marriage of a man and a woman. So, when all is said and done, let's all fight for our marriages for our

God intends us to enjoy them. We can surely have great enjoyable marriages. I have fought for mine and will continue to fight. Will you stand up and fight for yours?

#IsThereNotACause

CHAPTER 02

DEVOTION AND SURRENDER TO GOD

As we pledge to fight for our marriages, we must put things in order first. First things first!

Let's grasp these truths, become armed to the teeth in the fight and the devil will not prevail. First, let us acknowledge that marriage was authored and ordained by God, nothing more and nothing less! God is the inventor and manufacturer of this glorious thing called marriage – period! In fact, God is the manufacturer of the human race – period! These theories of evolution are nonsense according to me and according to the Bible which I believe with all my heart. How can we say we evolved from apes? My bible in Genesis 1 vs 26, 27 says, *"Then God said," Let Us make man in Our image, according to our likeness: Let them have dominion over the fish of the sea, over the birds of the air and over the cattle, over all the earth and over every creeping thing that creeps on the earth. Then God blessed them, and God said to them, "Be fruitful and multiply; fill the earth and subdue it; have dominion over the fish of the sea, over the birds of the air, and over every living thing that moves on the earth."* Genesis 2 vs 7 continues to say, *"And the Lord God formed man of the dust of the ground and breathed into his nostrils the breath of life and man became a living being."*

How can man then come from apes which according to the word of God we have dominion over? How can we evolve from something we have dominion over?

Let's set the facts right – man was created by God. As for me, the Bible clearly states I was created in the image of God not an ape. I am from God. What about you, are you from an ape?

Now as God created man (and woman) in His image stated in Genesis 1 vs 27, He also created marriage for the reasons given in the previous chapter and for procreation. Genesis 1 vs 28 says, *"Then God blessed them (man and woman – i.e. Adam and Eve) and God said to them "Be fruitful and multiply fill the earth and subdue it, have dominion over the fish of the sea, over the birds of the air and over every living thing that movies on the earth."* In Genesis 2 vs 21 – 24, the Bible describes how Eve (woman) was made and brought to Adam (man). Verse 23 describes how Adam is awed by this new being from his rib. Theirs is indeed an attraction and Adam calls her woman (in Hebrew - Ishshah). Verse 24 then states, *"Therefore a man shall leave his father and mother and be joined to his wife (female), and they shall become one flesh."* The first marriage was instituted by God Himself.

Now, when we consider the above truths, we realize that:
- a) Man was created (manufactured) by God.
- b) Marriage was created (instituted) by God.

YOUR MARRIAGE… HEAVEN OR HELL ON EARTH?

With this understanding that God is the manufacturer (originator) of both mankind and marriage, we surely must hear from him how to run and maintain this product called man, woman and the other one called marriage! Any manufacturer of a TV, sound system, vehicle, cell phone, always presents it with an operational manual. For mankind and marriage and all things that affect mankind, God gave us a more than reliable operational manual. We call it the Bible. The Bible was given to us as a manual to run our lives and our marriages. As manufacturers state in their manuals that if their product is not run according to its manual, the warranty becomes null and void – so is the case with mankind and marriages. If we don't run our lives or marriages according to God's plan and instructions that are clearly stated in the holy book, it's our fault when we crash, when we burn out, when we get messed up. As much as you CANNOT blame the manufacturer for non-compliance, we surely cannot blame God for our insolence and puffed-up pride when we ignore the manual and its author and try to run things our way.

If God said marriage is between man (male) and woman (female) who are we to try and change that and say marriage can be between two men or two women – that is from the pit of hell!

Now, for our lives and our marriages to run smoothly, we must surrender to God and cultivate a devotion to our maker both as couples, and singularly as individuals. When we come to marriage, the only help (whether directly or indirectly through people He sends) is our God – the creator of marriages. He created marriage not to fail. No one creates a product doomed to fail – at least no sober man does that, God has intended and intends marriage to prevail.

You and I, with our spouses must submit our lives to God. We must accept His son Jesus Christ into our lives. We must be filled with His Holy Spirit so that we can hear Him when He speaks and gives us direction either from His word (reading or from the preacher) or from that "still small voice". When we devote ourselves to be worshippers of Jehovah, He, God of Abraham, Isaac, and Jacob leads us and directs us in our marriages. He fights for us. We won't fight the devil on our own. God promises that when we surrender to be His, through accepting Jesus, He will never leave us nor forsake us. Hebrews 13 vs 5(b). God, through Christ and the power of the Holy Spirit in us has promised to fight our battles.

Daily devotion and surrender in prayer and attitudes to God allows Him to step in and fight for his "products". We also become sensitive in running our marriages. With the manual called the Bible in our hand (and reading it), with Jesus in our hearts and the power of God in us and on us (anointing) we are bound to win. The warranty is guaranteed to be honored.

Let husband and wife take up what's written in the word and apply it in their personal lives. This delivers us and improves us as individuals that we are easier to love, easier to talk to, easier to deal with, easier to simply live with. Let's devote ourselves and surrender to God and then devote ourselves to each other and surrender to each other. My marriage officer (Celebrant) – a great man of God, was given this word by the Lord at our wedding – John 12 vs 24 *"Most assuredly I say to you, unless a grain of wheat falls into the ground and dies, it remains alone. But if it dies, it produces much grain".* We therefore must die to self – submit and devote ourselves to God and submit and devote ourselves to each other in marriage.

YOUR MARRIAGE… HEAVEN OR HELL ON EARTH?

#NotIbutChristInMe

#NotMeButWe

CHAPTER

03

THE EARLY YEARS OF MARRIAGE

The early years in a relationship are the most vital in marriage. Unfortunately, most couples squander this time when both parties are still eager to impress and so are still "bendable", teachable, correctable, rebukeable. At this point neither of the two are set in their ways yet. They can still go this way or that. The uttermost and urgent agenda on each mind is not to disappoint the other and kill the romance. We are afraid of hurting each other's feelings so "we behave." The unfortunate thing is that it is also in this period that we sometimes hide from each other. We try to hide our weaknesses, so our spouses cannot easily help us deal with the issue. Everyone is trying to put "their best foot forward." But when we get used to each other more and more, we discover the angels we got married to are not angels after all. They rapidly lose their wings!

A joke is shared about a young Christian man who was attracted and taken by the wonderful, anointed singing of one sister in the praise and worship team. Whenever she sang, this young man's heart was always moved. So, he informed his counselor and his pastor that he wanted to marry that sister and he approached her and popped the question. Soon enough they had a wonderful wedding. But after some months, the euphoria faded away and the arguments set in. Strife was common, and he now saw this sister every day without makeup. So, after one of those not so good days they went to bed. He had trouble sleeping. The new wife on the other hand slept like a baby and was busy snoring. As the young man looked besides him at his (according to him) argumentative wife, no makeup – not really looking like she did when in the choir and snoring like a trombone, his heart sank, and he began to wonder why he married her in the first place. He remembered it was the singing that started it all. So, in trying to revive his ebbing feelings of love he shook her hard to wake her up. She was startled out of her deep sleep and asked her husband what was wrong, with panic written all over her face. All the young man could say and in a loud voice, half commanding and half begging was: "Sing, baby, sing! Please sing honey! Sing!" The poor lady was even confused – singing at 2 am? Why? Sing to who? Which song? And all the husband said over and over was: "Sing, I said sing baby! Please sing!"

From courtship onwards, a couple must start to discover each other and help each other. They must get a counselor to help them with pre-marital counseling where they start to deal with their weaknesses. Both should realize that they are not perfect. So, it is two imperfect beings trying to make the relationship work. When you discover that you are not perfect, you realize you can't judge your spouse to be. When you really love each other, love will cover a multitude of sins (1 Peter 4 vs 8). It means if you love someone, you are prepared to cover their weaknesses in the sense of not rejecting them but working with them to improve.

The common problem we face with young couples preparing for marriage is that most of them focus on the wrong thing. Most couples focus on the planning of the wedding and usually take a year or several months to plan it – to make it as flamboyant and as glamorous as possible. They are normally going for the so-called dream wedding or to outdo the most recent wedding of their peers. So, they spend most of the time and resources in planning the wedding instead of planning the marriage. The wedding is for a few hours and just one day, but the marriage must be for a lifetime. Our priorities are totally wrong as you can see. How can we spend twelve months planning a four- six-hour event and ignore a lifetime issue? Yet this is how most couples operate.

At a certain place in South Africa where Gwen and I were Overseers, God blessed us with several weddings. Young men and women started getting married. Single mothers got married. Couples who were traditionally married but had not exchanged marriage vows went on to have weddings and exchanged vows. For some who were just living together, after we counseled them, the husbands paid lobola and they wedded. We were there for four years, and God gave us grace to witness twelve, fourteen, sixteen and seventeen weddings progressively for those four years. It was really the grace of God. What I want to bring forward is this – with seventeen weddings in one year (January to December) we had to do a lot of pre-marital counseling. My wife and I are passionate about this. Seeing that there were so many couples needing counseling, we decided to have premarital counseling classes. So nearly every Sunday after service, the couples intending to marry would attend classes where Gwen and I took turns to teach them and have question and answer sessions. By the time these couples wedded we would have taught and imparted quite a lot of marriage insights into them and thus they would hit the ground running.

We would also free them from the notion of holding a glamorous wedding that would leave them in debt and starting their new life together with debts from the wedding. It is always better to have a wedding you can really afford. It is the exchange of vows before God and the church which is important. People soon forget how glamorous the wedding was, and soon enough someone will outdo you. Therefore, it is better to have enough money to go for a nice, decent honeymoon. Then, during the honeymoon – it's not about sex only, discuss your future. Share your dreams. Gently correct each other and set your boundaries from the onset. If those boundaries are not godly, remove them. Those that can be moved – move them. (We will talk about boundaries in another chapter later).
As a young couple if you do not work out your issues early in your marriage it is going to be harder later. As each spouse corrects the other, the corrected spouse may take it as an attack. They will be wondering why suddenly after a year or two you do not like this or that, or you are complaining about this or that when you have been quiet all along. Better deal with issues while both parties are still "bendable" and eager to please and impress each other.

My spiritual father, Apostle Dr. Ezekiel H. Guti taught us a long time ago that issues must be dealt with earlier on in marriage. It will cause your marriage to quickly mature and be strong. You will enjoy later - even for life, the hard work of the early days. I took this to heart and started to apply it in my marriage. I am the type of guy who when he hears a teaching – he wants to implement it immediately for maximum effect. So, in the early days, as much as our relationship was vibrant, Gwen and I got time to really get into it and talk things out. There were arguments. There were tears (I call them 'waterworks' – a term affectionately borrowed from my late father-in-law). There were late nights due to talking things out. Apostle Dr. Ezekiel H. Guti had also taught us never to go to bed with an unresolved issue. I took that literally. My wife would try to sleep while she was angry, moody, or sulking and I would wake her up to talk things over. She would try to sleep and cover her head, but I would uncover her head, grab her by her shoulders, and sit her up in bed. We had to talk things over. It was not abuse. Soon enough she realized that if you were ever to get some sleep, the sooner she poured out her heart and we talked and reconciled the better. You see, my wife is an introvert, and everyone knows that introverts do not usually talk much. But I would not allow that to ruin my marriage. Since those early years, we do not go to bed angry at each other or with an issue unresolved. We iron it out before bed.

It is important for both sides to nip bad character and bad habits in the bud in those early years. One such incident was so humorous that we still laugh about it. You see, my wife would try to control me or manipulate me with her tears. But her dad had forewarned me to watch out for – as he called it "waterworks". Secondly, Gwen was clearly her dad's favorite. The father loved her so much he would do almost anything for her – and she knew it! She had a rather harsh childhood due to a situation in her life that needed prolonged medical attention and Dad was always there for her. They had built such a bond. Then in comes dear me into the life of dear Gwendolene Nothando Tendayi – daddy's favorite. The first few months I didn't know what to do. She would always make me feel bad and cause me to let her have her way by her always comparing me with her father. She would go, "My Dad would have done such and such for me", "My Dad would have bought me this", "My Dad... my Dad."

YOUR MARRIAGE… HEAVEN OR HELL ON EARTH?

This continued until I was sick and tired of it. So, one day while I was at work I did a short prayer and said, "God, help me with this situation at home. This must end." God is faithful. He gave me a revelation. So as soon as I got home, I put my stuff in the bedroom and went straight to the lounge. My wife was in the kitchen. I called her to the lounge and asked her to sit on the sofa directly opposite me. She was obviously very surprised because we usually always sat next to each other cuddling and so forth, but at this moment I meant business. Someone had to be delivered that day!
So, she sat on the assigned sofa. She probably sensed a difference in my mood and behavior, causing her to look at the floor. I asked her to look at me and she looked for a short while, and then back at the floor – confused about what I was up to. I insisted that she look at me with a very firm voice and so she did. When she did, I said, "Take a good look at me. Do you really see me?" She nodded yes. Then I said again, "Yeah, look at me closely." With her eyes fully focused on me I said, "You are seeing me clearly – right? Tell me, do I look like your father? Do I? Your father is tall, I am short. Your father is dark in complexion, and I am light skinned. Your father is a high school English teacher, I am not a teacher, I am an Air Traffic Controller. I am not your father, and I will never be your father! So, stop comparing me with your father!" Immediately she burst out laughing and I laughed with her, and that was the end of it all. She never ever compared me with her father again. Whenever we talk of this day, we burst out laughing. The point is that I nipped the problem in the bud those early months. No man likes to be compared with another.

Early days in marriage must be both full of fun, sex, and a lot of work. If you do not work on your marriage and mature, you can be married for five years, ten years, but you will still experience the troubles of a one year, two year-old marriage.

The 2 stages of Romantic love

According to Dr Gary Chapman in his book, "Things I wish I'd known Before We Got Married" - © 2010 pp 22-24, he states the fact that romantic love has 2 stages:

1st Stage (Euphoric Stage)
This is the "being in love" stage. Euphoric feelings take over. You are beside yourself with love. Your lover seems perfect. He/she can do no wrong. You cannot even identify character flaws. Even if parents, relatives, or friends point out issues with your lover, you say they do not understand or are outright jealous. At this stage, which may last up to two years, you feel the person you love is the center of your universe. When at college, your grades can even fall. Who cares about studying when you are in love?

2nd Stage (Reality Stage)
The Euphoric stage is followed by the reality stage. You realize your lover or spouse is not an angel. You need to really make an effort to keep your love emotional. Loving becomes intentional and not just automatic.

I am persuaded to think that it is at the realistic level where each spouse is now also out of their shells. They are more vocal, more critical, more prone to argue. Doubt can even set in whether he/she is the right one or you wonder if you made a mistake? What you need to realize is that true love is not a feeling. True love is a commitment. Feelings come and go. Love stays forever. It just changes from the goose bumps all over feeling to commitment and being intentional.

My suggestion, therefore, is for a couple to know beforehand that the euphoric stage will soon pass. But when you have the right teaching, you do not allow the euphoric stage to blind you so much you do not look out for issues that need to be worked on in your relationship, on your partner or on yourself. If we can work things out at the euphoric stage, it is easier because we are very long suffering with each other. Work out your social, spiritual, intellectual goals in time. Check if you have the same core value systems. Just being in love is not enough to build a marriage. There are many couples who love each other but are divorced now.

Work it out and work it out early. Talk, communicate, be frank.

#Ididn'tKnowHeSnoresAndBreaksWindInBed

CHAPTER

04

COMMUNICATION IN MARRIAGE

There are four most problematic areas in marriage, namely – communication, sex, money, and in-laws.

Of these four, communication is the most important, for the rest depend on it. If your communication as a couple is sound, then you can work out issues of sex, money, and in-laws without much drama.

We will dedicate this chapter to communication: Proverbs 15 v 1 advises, *"A soft answer turns away wrath, but a harsh word stirs up anger."*

What is communication?
I will describe communication as an exchange of information, feelings, thoughts, and emotions - both vocal and non-vocal. A wink, a smile, a sigh, a smirk, a frown, a nod, or a shake of the head means something. Body language is a big part of communication, the folding of arms when the other party is speaking for example, can

mean you are talking to yourself over there – I am closed over here. Or it can be, go ahead, let us see what you want to do or what you can do.

A major part of communication is listening. It takes both parties to listen and not just talk. In my counseling of couples over the years, I have realized that as couples, we miss each other as we fail to listen. Each party wants to speak their mind, put in their point or grievance at all costs. So, we fail to hear the spouse trying to put across their issue, their source of pain or grievance. So, there is much talking but no communication because we are not listening to each other. It is true that we must listen more and talk less. This is why God gave us two ears but one mouth! James 1 vs 19 says, *"So then, my beloved brethren let every man be swift to hear, slow to speak, slow to wrath."*

As a couple, we must always communicate clearly from the time before the wedding to ever after! None of the two must assume that the other knows what they are thinking or feeling or what they intend to do. No-one is a mind reader. One American brother said that women get angry about things they think the husband ought to do, or to have done yet it was never communicated to the husband. He said ladies must know men might have ESPN (sports channel) but surely, we do not have ESP (Extra Sensory Perception).

When a couple does not communicate, there are always surprises of a nasty kind in that marriage. I have known husbands who buy cars, sell houses, and invest lots of money or even lend it without communicating to their wives. Fireworks (of the nasty kind) ensue, without fail! I have also known wives who spend money or buy some big things without a nod from the man because they never communicated.

My background is in Aviation (Air Traffic Control). Now in aviation, in particular, air traffic control – communication is vital. This is communication between two airports or air spaces who are handing over air traffic to each other, or communication between the pilot and air traffic control. This is why there is a phonetic alphabet that we use and a certain way we pronounce and call numbers – all for clarity in communication. The words "over", "roger", "out", "CAVOK" mean something distinct to the aviator. The International Civil Aviation Organization (ICAO), the world aviation governing body, has had to change some phrases to ensure safety when such phrases have caused confusion before. In the past, aircraft have collided due to lack of communication or unclear communication.

Thus, each pilot or each air traffic controller MUST always acknowledge receipt of the message the other one has transmitted and, in some cases, repeat the same message (read back). For example, when air traffic control gives the pilot the atmospheric pressure, runway to land, departure route and flight level, the pilot ALWAYS has to read back in case he copied wrong and will end up colliding with another aircraft. So, to me this is a big issue. Therefore, I have trained my wife to always acknowledge when we communicate. I want to know if she heard my communication clearly to avoid drama later. Have you ever seen a husband or wife who says something to their spouse and assumes the spouse has heard only to discover the other party misheard and did something else.

When a spouse does not communicate with their partner, it causes confusion and insecurities that breed trouble. When the husband and wife do not communicate well enough that each one's feelings are emptied out, that spouse will confide in and communicate with someone at work, gym, or other places. This can be the beginning of extra marital affairs. When a spouse feels they are not being listened to or given attention, they will look for a listening ear at work and an emotional affair starts which nearly always ends up as a full-blown adulterous affair. It is wrong for a married man or woman to bare his/her soul to a "friend" at work, yet it happens often. Also, there are men who communicate more with their mothers than with their wives. That is very wrong! Your wife is obviously the number one person in your life, yet she may end up hearing her husband's plans from his mother or family members – it is wrong. Some wives have remained under the thumb of their dads or brothers – it should never be like that.

Husband and wife must be one. This comes about through a lot of sharing, a lot of openness – a lot of communication. There must be no secrets between husband and wife. Genesis 2 vs 25 says this about Adam and Eve, *"they were both naked and were not ashamed"*. I am persuaded to think that the nakedness went beyond a physical lack of clothes but that they were also transparent with each other. A good marriage is built on trust. Trust is built on understanding and confidence in one's partner. That understanding of each other comes from much communication with each other. When a disagreement or argument happens between a couple, they must fight "clean". Every marriage will have disagreements – let no one fool you! It is how you solve the issue without animosity and violence that matters. Arguments or "intense moments of fellowship" as Gwen and I call them – will arise. Your communication must be great to be able to handle these safely, maturely, and comfortably.

Here are some ground rules my wife and I have set and have adhered to for over thirty-five years. We call them "Rules of Engagement":

1. No yelling or screaming – that is not communication.

2. No swearing or cursing.
3. No name calling.
4. No threats of violence.
5. No threat of divorce i.e. I will leave/divorce you OR I will chase you away (Proverbs18 vs 21).
6. No "Intense fellowship" in the presence of our children or in public.
7. No cheap shots – like bringing something your spouse said in confidence or vulnerable moment in the past into the present argument.

Here are other rules of "fighting clean" that we have taught in the past:
1. Keep to the subject at hand – solve THIS issue not others that come by "revelation".
2. Stop being historical i.e., do not bring a list of issues from the past.
3. Stop being hysterical – control your emotions and voice.
4. Never say something negative about your spouse's relatives even if he/she does. Remember blood is thicker than water. She will forget she name-called her sister, but if you joined in, she will remember that and conclude you dislike her relatives.
5. Always fight to win your spouse and your marriage and not the argument. Remember you can win the argument but lose your partner and your marriage.

One important thing the wives need to note very well is that most men do not shout or show an intensity when they correct or rebuke you. Do not take that to be a sign of weakness or that he does not mean what he is saying because he has said it so casually. Have ears that hear! As men, we hate repeating ourselves. So, when your hubby tells you to stop something – stop it immediately. Many women have lost their marriages because they only discovered when it was too late that the husband meant it. In his book, "Wise man, (page)" Apostle Dr. Ezekiel H. Guti said, "The other problem I have learnt from some women and through this problem they have lost their marriages: Do you want to know the problem? They don't have a sensitive heart. When the husband says," I don't like this" – they take it lightly, they think it's just news not knowing that the husband is serious and wants the wife to change. They don't understand when the man says I don't like this, or I am not happy about this ... They will only know when the husband is no longer coming home at the right time... I have seen separation and divorces because women don't act on what he says... If you don't want to lose your marriage, please wake up and listen."

Another communication problem ladies must watch out for, so they stop doing it is nagging and constant argument. When you nag and argue a lot, the husband can "switch off" and though you continue talking no one is listening to you. The problem is that he gets used to your nagging, finding fault and complaining that the day you will have something genuine, something important, something that makes sense, he will not listen thinking, She's at it again!" You may get into trouble as a family because the husband did not listen to, because he assumed you were being your usual self - jabbering on for nothing. However, on the other hand, if you are of a quiet spirit and only speak strongly when there is a genuine issue, when you do speak, he listens and saves the day because he thinks this lady normally does not talk this much – it must be important. So, sisters – as Gwen (my wife) says – "Save your gun powder".

Here are some scriptures that truly resonate with what I have been saying:

Proverbs 19 vs 13 – *"A foolish son is the ruin of his father, and the contentions of a wife are a continual dripping."*

Proverbs 21 vs 9 – *"Better to dwell in a corner of a housetop than in a house shared with a contentious woman."*

Proverbs 21 vs 19 – *"Better to dwell in the wilderness than with a contentious and angry woman."*

Proverbs 27 vs 15-16 – *"A continual dripping on a rainy day and a contentious woman are alike, whoever restrains her restrains the wind, and grasps oil with his right hand!"*

Warning to men

On average, men are worse communicators than women. This is because as men, we grow up with macho teachings that a man must not show emotion – and a man must "suffer quietly" and stand the heat. We are told that a real man keeps his cards close to his chest, but this becomes problematic in marriage. The wife expects the husband to talk to her about issues at his job, his plans for the family and life in general. But not having learnt to communicate effectively, the man ends up going solo as a "lone ranger" in some things.

The problem with this is both the wife and children may seem to be fighting him when it is not the case. I have heard men complain that their wives do not support their vision and plans for the family. But when you ask the wife, you realize she is not aware of any vision or plan. Most men fail to articulate their vision and plans to their wives for the wives to understand and grasp the vision and run side by side with the husband. A woman cannot support what she does not know. Friction arises under such circumstances. For example, a sudden cut in grocery and entertainment money by the husband gets the madam and the children up in arms even though there may be an excellent reason behind it. The husband may have a five-year plan (which is great) for saving money and buying land to build or deposit for a house. He would have done his calculations already but neglected to inform the family clearly. Suddenly the wife hears that groceries are to be cut in half – no more ice cream and other luxuries. No more hair salon allowance and the like. Surely such a man is playing with his own life! The wife can influence the kids too – no ice cream, no holidays, no good Christmas spending – that is a recipe for disaster! Yet it is very possible to achieve the savings and the final goal through thorough communication. All he must do is sit the wife down and download to her the blueprint of his vision, the calculations and how to get there. Allow her to contribute her ideas too. As she buys into your vision, she does not fight you because it is clear to her, and she helps you convince the children as well. She tells them dad is an excellent administrator and has planned for us to have our own house, and this is how we will get there. So, the wife becomes a real help mate as the bible says, not a hindrance. She even rallies up the children to save up on electricity, water and stop demanding pizza and McDonalds every other day. Even the bible illustrates what I am saying, Habakkuk 2 vs 2 says, *"Then the LORD answered me and said, 'Write the vision and make it plain on tablets that he may run who reads it".* Yes, my brother, write that vision – write it big in her mind and see how much she will support you. Also, the husband must also listen to the wife. She is your helpmate. Genesis 21 v 12 states, *"whatever Sara has said to you, listen to her voice".* What both husband and wife must remember is that any communication can be improved. As we mature in marriage so must our communication.

Experts say there are five levels of communication. I will list them below with a brief description. We will start from the lowest level and proceed to end with the best – level one. Check what level you are on with your spouse:

Five Levels of Communication

Level 5 – Cliché Conversation (small talk)
It is shallow; no feelings, no emotions – conversation bordering on meaningless, with questions like: "How are you?", "How was work?", "How are things going?" It is considered better than awkward, embarrassing silence; but is boring, frustrating and does not build.

Level 4 – Factual Conversation
You share information but no personal comments or feelings. You may even talk about the neighbors who bought a new car. Or worse, the husband grabs his car keys and puts on a jacket and the wife asks, "Where are you going?", "Out", he says. Men are chief culprits here, but unfortunately modern women are fast functioning on this level as well.

Level 3 – Sharing ideals (and Opinions)
Intimacy begins here. Sharing of thoughts, feelings, and opinions. It is good if the partner answers well and makes it safe for the other to continue without fear of being hurt as he/she is making themselves vulnerable. If handled well, things can improve.

Level 2 Feelings and emotions
Pretty good, gut level communication. Sharing of feelings and emotions. Verbalize all that is inside you. Give and take. Insightful if the sharing is reciprocal. Spouse feels safe, accepted, and listened to.

Level 1 Peak (Deep Insight)
Perfectly in tune. Symphony of the soul. Sharing with absolute honesty, transparency, depth, openness and in some cases measures of "telepathy". You think alike – sometimes at the same time. Can end up finishing each other's sentences.

What level are you?
Ezekiel Type of communication
And yet there is another level of communication. We call it the Ezekiel type of communication. In Ezekiel 3 vs 15 the bible reads, "Then I came to the captives at Tel Abib who dwelt by the River Chebar; and I sat where they sat and remained there astonished among them for seven days."

Here we see Prophet Ezekiel being sent by God to prophesy to the Jews who were in captivity. But Ezekiel did not just go to the Jews and start to say "Thus saith the Lord." He came among them, sat where they sat astonished at what was going on with his countrymen. He sat there for seven days before he started prophesying what he had been sent. Sitting among his countrymen for seven days enabled him to assess and appreciate their plight and situation. It meant that as he prophesied after that, he understood who he was prophesying to. He could communicate with empathy and understanding because he had taken time to be with them so his communication would be most effective.

This happens in marriage. People who marry normally come from different backgrounds, but with enough communication and each spouse getting into the shoes of the other, they will understand their spouse. There must be some getting into each other's shoes – feel what it is like. For example, a husband might have grown up without his biological mother who passed on when he was very young. An aunty, mother's sister, could have taken him in – or his paternal uncle's wife could have taken him in and nurtured him just like a mother and so his attachment to her is that of a mother and son. The wife of this husband must know exactly how her husband feels about this aunt. This is because he may want to sacrifice and send her a big amount of money for one reason or another. To the wife, he may look like he is wasting money because people do not normally send aunts a lot of money. The wife thinks he surely has no mother to support and so must not be sending money, yet to him the aunt is his mother in every way – with all the mother-son emotional attachments. The wife must be in his position to understand this so that she does not start a fight, because according to her, he is sending lots of money to a mere aunt and yet to him he is sending it to his mother. The wife, through communication about the husband's background should "sit where he sits" and realize the bond he has with this aunt he calls his mother. If the wife fails to understand this or vice versa there is going to be some fighting. So, both parties must always get into each other's shoes to have the very best understanding of the situations.

The 5 Languages of Love
Family psychologist and bestselling author Dr Gary Chapman – author of several books, has written a book called "The 5 Love Languages." That book is a powerful tool for communication in marriage, more so for communicating love.

Gwen and I have incorporated this resource into our Couples Seminars and Retreats with astounding results, as couples learn to understand each other better.

YOUR MARRIAGE... HEAVEN OR HELL ON EARTH?

The gist of the book is that in a relationship, communication of love differs from person to person depending on how he/she is wired. In other words, they can only understand and accept that you love them if you communicate to them in a certain way – their love language. It is very interesting to know not only your love language, but vital to know your spouse's love language. This means to say when you know your spouse's love language, love him/her by communicating in his/her love language.

Let us get into an exercise to see what your love language is and more importantly, your spouse's love language.
Here are the 5 Love Languages by Dr. Gary Chapman: Note that an individual can have more than one love language:

1. **Physical Touch** – The spouse feels loved when you touch him/her – an embrace, a hug, holding of hands, a rub on the thigh when seated together, a rub on the shoulder, a rub on the arm, a pat on the bums (discreetly of course) and even making love. Needless to say, this is my primary language.
2. **Receiving Gifts** – he/she says if you love me, show me by buying me gifts. He /she expects something rather often than not. Some perfume, a good book, a necklace, a ring, flowers and other gifts.
3. **Acts of Service** – the greatest thing you can do for me to show your love – they say, serve me. Help with cooking or doing the dishes, mopping or vacuuming, taking out the trash, making a cup of tea or coffee and other acts of service.
4. **Quality Time** – these individuals with this love language say, if you love me, spend quality time with me – no distractions. Away with the iPad and phone! No TV, nobody else. Maybe dinner, a picnic, a leisurely walk in the park, a coffee and

cake in a hidden corner, a weekend getaway, a seven day or some weeks holidays, just the two of us.
5. **Words of Affirmation** – this is when the partner with this love language wants you to affirm, acknowledge and show appreciation when they do good. Vocalize your thanks or appreciation of their cooking. For example, the way they keep the house clean, their makeup, their dressing, their hard work and anything that might be worthwhile. Some may even love a letter (note) an email or text message of your appreciation. They feel good and loved when you affirm them.

Power of Apology
Communication breakdown can arise when we wrong each other and fail to apologize adequately. Part of the reason is that, like the languages of love, we also have languages of apology. In other words, the aggrieved party may feel the other party is not serious in their apology because he/she did not get the type of apology that works for him/her. Surely grieving each other in marriage we do, and we will do – but we must be quick to set things right. It is good to vocalize your apology. We all make mistakes, and we are also wronged. What is important is to quickly forgive. Gwen and I teach forgiveness in marriage, and we say if you cannot forgive, do not get married.

Quite often in our seminars people ask who must say sorry first – the husband or the wife? Our answer is – the more mature one. It takes guts and maturity to own your mistake and apologize, let alone to apologize when it is you who has been wronged. Yes, there are times when the aggrieved will apologize to maintain peace and also keep the communication channel open. The small word, "sorry" is very precious and healing work. We wish we could use it more often.

However, according to Dr Chapman, sometimes the words "I am sorry" just do not cut it. This is because each one of us has a language of apology – something within the apology that makes us feel the one at fault is truly sorry. So here are "The 5 Apology Languages" by Dr. Gary Chapman and Jennifer Thomas:

The 5 Apology Languages
1. Express regret - "I am sorry" must be accompanied with what you are sorry for. Alone, the statement "I am sorry" is too general for some. People of this language want to hear what you are sorry for. It comforts them to know that you know where you have erred e.g. I am sorry I broke my promise to take you out tonight.
2. Accepting Responsibility - you indicate that you were wrong and go on to explain your wrong behavior and accept your responsibility.
3. Making Restitution - this is when your spouse's language of apology demands that you show that you are indeed remorseful, make amends, correct the situation, do something.
4. Genuinely expressing the desire to change your behavior - the "I am sorry" must come with a solution to keep the bad behavior from recurring. In this case the aggrieved party wants to know what you are going to do to stop recurrence of the situation.
5. Requesting forgiveness- this is when the injured spouse wants to hear the other say "Will you please forgive me?" This is good to hear to those whose primary language of apology is requesting forgiveness. In their minds if you are sincere, you will ask them to forgive you. Your requesting forgiveness touches their heart.

Residue in a bottle

Not dealing with issues, that is, not talking about them creates a time bomb. Let each issue be exhausted or it will be like residue dregs that fill a bottle. A marriage can only take unresolved issues to a certain level before an explosion takes place.

We cannot conclude this chapter on communication without talking about the killers or hindrances of communication. That is what we will tackle next.

Communication Killers

Communication between a couple may be hindered by the following factors:

1. Fear of rejection – if I voice my honest opinion, what will my spouse say? How will he/she react? Won't he/she love me less? Or say bad words that will hurt me? This leads to a lack of honesty.
2. The Messiah Mask – This is when a spouse moves around with a "holy mask" outside the home. He appears to be an angel at church and elsewhere but at home he/she is unapproachable. Everyone else out there thinks he is a "messiah" but at home he/she is a person who incites terror and intimidation, "a terrorist". No one can talk to him/her freely.
3. Volcanic Response – Proverbs 15 vs 1 states, *"A soft answer turns away wrath, but a harsh word stirs up anger"* and Proverbs 29 vs 11 goes on to say, *"A fool vents all his feelings, but a wise man holds them back."*
   A Volcanic Response is when one partner mentions something and because the other spouse does not want it discussed he/she erupts like a volcano – a real Mt. Etna!

There is shouting, intimidation and temper tantrums. This usually happens when you are about to get to the truth of a matter and the partner is afraid to be found out. You are too close to the truth, so they use this trick to control or manipulate their spouse. The spouse will normally shut up to avoid a ruckus. This is a real and cruel communication killer.

4. Tears – Waterworks! Rivers of Babylon! Victoria Falls! Niagara Falls! Or whatever you want to call them. Also used to manipulate and control when you get close to the truth of a matter. Tries to stop the other spouse from digging deeper on an issue.

This is one of the most favorite tricks of a control freak.

5. Silence – You speak, you do not get an answer. She/he wants you to change the subject. It is a sign of passive anger – passive aggression. It is the opposite of the volcano but with the same effect. They may try to enhance this by banging the door, folding of arms, humming a tune like you are not even there – even rolling of eyes! As kids say, "Talk to my hand because the face ain't listening". This silence can go on for days.

The above five things surely do hinder a couple's communication.

#TwoEarsButOneMouth

#ListenMoreAndTalkLess

CHAPTER

05

SEX – LET'S TALK ABOUT IT

Sex is an integral part of marriage. It is very important, so important that after a wedding there is talk of consummation of the marriage – that is sex. Sex has been talked about everywhere else except in church, and that is fast changing. Children of God have found out that they have allowed the devil and his cohorts to lead the way on this subject – that is bringing out a skewed view of sex. From the onset let us remember that sex is of God. Sex was created by God for his people in marriage. The sexual organs (master pieces they are, I must add) were created by God. The orgasm or big "O" as some call it, was created by God. The devil cannot create. Satan never created and will never create. There is only one Creator, Jehovah God Almighty. The devil only takes what God has created and corrupts and prostitutes it. Satan perverts and has perverted sex through prostitution, fornication, adultery, homosexuality, pornography, bestiality, incest and all the disgusting sex acts that operate outside the sanctity of the marriage bed of a man and woman in holy matrimony.

YOUR MARRIAGE… HEAVEN OR HELL ON EARTH?

Sex is good! Sex is great! But ONLY in the safe confines of marriage. God has created things that are good for us if they are operated in their place. Fire in a fireplace brings warmth and cooks food. Outside its designated confines, it burns down the house, the house next door, the factories, and forests. Water is also good in its designated "containers" where we use it to drink, bath, cook – even in the rivers and oceans where it is vital for the survival of fish and other marine life. Outside its confines or boundaries, water becomes floods, tsunamis and so forth and becomes a killer. In the same vein, sex outside marriage is disastrous. In this chapter, we are going to discuss sex in holy matrimony as its Creator, God Almighty meant it to be. We must begin by denying and disproving the myth that the sin Adam and Ever committed in Eden was sexual intercourse. NO! According to the Bible, the fall of man (Adam) is in Genesis Chapter 3, but in the very first chapter (Genesis 1 vs 28), God had already said to Adam and Eve, *"Be fruitful and multiply, fill the earth and subdue it."* How were they to multiply and fill the earth if they were not going to have sexual intercourse? So, it is clear that the fall of Adam and Eve was as the word of God says – eating of the forbidden tree of the knowledge of good and evil, nothing more, nothing less! In Genesis 4 vs 1, the bible says, *"Now Adam knew his wife and she conceived"* and verse 25 says, *"And Adam knew his wife again and she bore a son and named him Seth"*.

Now it is clear that sex was not the cause of the fall. God created sexual organs on both Adam and Eve and told them to go and multiply. Multiplication, as seen in Genesis 4 vs 1 and 25 could only happen through sex. This is why these same scriptures do NOT say, "And Adam committed sin with Eve", but Adam "knew" Eve – Hebrew word "Yada", meaning knowing intimately through intercourse. So now that the myth is out of the way, let us discuss sex. As we are now on the same page, understand that God gave sex to humankind as a blessing and as a means for procreation – that is, multiplication. God is a good God. God is a very good God and ALL He does is good. James 1 vs 17 says, "Every good gift and every perfect gift is from above and comes down from the Father of lights, with whom there is no variation or shadow of turning".

Now, sex, if mishandled in marriage, can lead to divorce. It is the desire of God that a husband and wife enjoy their sexual relationship. It is God who gave us the sex drive (libido). All we need to do is to practise self-control and not use that libido outside the marriage. A certain Jewish Rabbi wrote that there has been an imbalance on sex in this world. God made it balanced, but the devil hijacked it, perverted it, and made it dirty through the sinful acts we mentioned earlier. The devil took it so far to the left – devilish he made it to be. On the other hand, the church tried to bring it to the right, but took it too far to the right, where enjoying sex especially for married women was taken to be immoral. For them, sex became a drag. It was just for procreation. It became a necessary evil. However, in the dark ages church elders were known to secretly visit brothels and having mistresses where they could enjoy unbridled escapades of sexual bouts – as there was nothing exciting at home. So, they became hypocrites, and the marriage bed was defiled.

It is with renewal in the church and the revival of the reading and understanding of scriptures that children of God started to see sex in its perfection and enjoy it as God meant it to be. Sex is to be enjoyed, without hangups – religious or traditional. Now let us see what the New Testament says about sex. We take it from 1 Corinthians 7.

YOUR MARRIAGE… HEAVEN OR HELL ON EARTH?

I Corinthians 7 vs 1 – 5 & 9: *"Now concerning the things of which you wrote to me:*
It is good for a man not to touch a woman. Nevertheless, because of sexual immorality, let each man have his own wife, and let each woman have her own husband. Let the husband render to his wife the affection due her, and likewise also the wife to her husband. The wife does not have authority over her own body, but the husband does. And likewise, the husband does not have authority over his own body, but the wife does. Do not deprive one another except with consent for a time, that you may give yourselves to fasting and prayer; and come together again so that Satan does not tempt you because of your lack of self-control."
Verse 9 – *"but if they cannot exercise self-control, let them marry. For it is better to marry than to burn with passion"*.

Paul writes to the Corinthian church about things they had written to him about. He says if a man does not want to get involved with a woman it is "cool" – but because of the danger of sexual immorality, let a man have his own wife and a wife her own husband. Now verse 3 is key – he says that a husband must give his wife her sexual rights and vice versa the wife to the husband. In verse 4, both wife and husband do not own their bodies anymore, but through marriage they own each other's bodies now. Verse 5 says do not deprive each other of sex except briefly by agreement to fast and pray but have sex soon again so that Satan does not tempt you through lack of self-control. In verse 9 Paul says if the unmarried cannot exercise self-control, let them marry rather than burn with passion. See that he is not condemning the passion, but simply that it must be within marriage. I suppose this is clear enough that sex in marriage is of God and that it must be enjoyed.

At the time of writing this book, my wife and I have been married for thirty-five years. It has been thirty-five years of sweet and passionate sex in holy matrimony. But in the early days as much as I enjoyed the sex, I was guilt ridden every time after sex because of the type of life I had lived before the Lord Jesus saved me. However, I got delivered by the Word of God. Unfortunately, there are husbands and wives who are failing to enjoy the marriage bed because of their past. If you are born again, you are a new creature – allow Jesus to deliver you so you can enjoy sex with your spouse. Later in this chapter we shall talk about things that hinder married couples' sexual pleasure.

Deprive not one another!

As we read in 1 Corinthians 7 above, husband and wife must NEVER say "no" to each other on sex. Depriving your spouse of sex is a sin. Verse 5 says deprive not one another – so depriving one another is disobeying the Word of God and disobeying God's word is a sin. Churches are full of people, especially women...and a few men too, who are sinners in this area. What the bible says is not a suggestion but a commandment. How else do you want God to say it? We may be powerful men and women of God yet sinning in this area. Deprive not one another! Generally, men have a higher sex drive than women and that makes men to want sex more often. But this does not mean women do not like sex. They do, but most women's sex drive is less, though when aroused they can become very enthusiastic about it. A husband must never have to beg for sex from his wife and vice versa. In our couples' seminars, we have heard questions like; "How many times should a couple have sex in a week?" Or "Who determines the frequency of sex?" Answer: "A couple can have sex as many times a week or a day as they wish. Secondly, the spouse with the higher sex drive should be allowed to determine the frequency." No man and no woman must be reduced to be a beggar of sex. The problem is if the other spouse is not being satisfied sexually, problems arise.

Here is a list of problems that arise when one spouse is kept sex starved:
1) Adultery – a child who cannot eat at home ends up eating at a neighbor's house.
2) Fights and quarrels – sex starved individuals can be unpleasant to each other, and to other people. They are also prone to fights as a couple.
3) Moods and cruelty towards the depriver.
4) Breakdown in communication – it is hard even to reason with a man with an erection!
5) Suspicions – "If he isn't giving me sex, he is giving someone else somewhere".
6) Ill feelings and vindictiveness towards the withholding spouse.
7) Lack of blessing – even financially (God blesses a happy united family...and sex brings spiritual unity).
8) Lack of a sense of well-being.
9) Revenge – "fixing" or being spiteful to each other in other areas where the deprived has power e.g., money.
10) Divorce – this is sad but true. We have seen it too many times. Almost all people who marry take sex to be part of the marriage deal. When they do not get the sex, they ask themselves, "so why should I stay in this sexless marriage?"

This is what the devil wants to happen. In the marriage vows there is a pledge where each spouse says, "And with my body I will honor you" – so what happened? It is a trick of the devil through ignorance or demonic influence. We have seen the devil at work in this area –

fighting couples not to enjoy sex. To see that it is the devil, do you realize how as pastors we fight to keep young adults in courtship to remain pure? They cannot keep their hands off each other. Some end up under discipline at church as they fall into fornication. Check out the same couple a few years after they wed, and you see that the opposite is true. The devil now fights to keep this married couple from having sex. The wife rehearses 1001 excuses not to have sex or the husband is always too tired to give sex to his wife, or he cannot get an erection.

We have even dealt with demonic activity in this area. Wives having spiritual husbands that sleep with them and so they have no interest in sleeping with their real husbands and vice versa. Men who only experience an erection away from their wives and when the wife is present, are unable to get an erection. I have seen demons that cause erectile dysfunctions being casted out of men. Some erectile dysfunction is medical – but still has its original source as the devil. Women who get terribly sick when they are approached for sex by their spouses. Backaches, headaches, itchy vagina – this is not an exhaustive list. There are times when the husband cannot penetrate his wife like she is a virgin, when she has given birth and has three children already! A demon closes the vaginal canal to cause pain and a reluctance to have sex. Sometimes when a couple plans to have sex, a big fight just erupts from nowhere so that in the end no one is in the mood for sex and so there is no intimacy.

Benefits of sex

The devil fights hammer and tongs to stop you from having sex with your spouse because he knows if you enjoy your marriage, you and your wife will be better believers and a mighty weapon in the hands of the Almighty. Remember marriage is a picture of Christ and the church and I have seen it being used by God as an evangelistic tool. Godly and happy marriages attract people who desire the same – who are tired of the same old, same old, and so you can point them to Christ.

The benefits of sex in marriage are enormous: spiritually, physically, mentally, and socially.

Here are some of the benefits of sex:
1) Sex brings the couple together to be really one, *"The two shall become one flesh"* Genesis 2 vs 24, Matthew 19 vs 5, Ephesians 5 vs 31, Mark 10 vs 6-8, 1 Corinthians 6 vs 16. Of special note is 1 Corinthians 6 vs 16 which states, *"Or do you not know that he who is joined to a harlot (has sex with a prostitute) is one body with her? For "the two"* he says, *"shall become one flesh"*. Therefore, if sex with a harlot makes you one with the harlot, it also means that sex with your spouse makes you one with your spouse.
2) Sex in marriage fosters a bond and strengthens that bond spiritually, physically, and emotionally. It brings deep unity, and this unity brings the blessing of God for "there the Lord will command a blessing – life forever more" (Psalms 133 vs 3b). Couples bond through sex.
3) Sex in marriage promotes emotional stability and peace of mind – a sense of well-being. A good bout of sex equals some exercises that boost physical and mental health.
4) Regular sex reduces stress, depression, and bolsters self-esteem.

5) Sex releases hormones into the body – chemicals like dopamine and oxytocin that bring good feelings and a sense of warmth and fuzziness.
6) Sex has been proved to ward off colds and flu.
7) Sex is known to improve brain power – ability to remember and to improve analytical thinking.
8) It improves overall fitness. Yes, regular sex can improve your physical fitness. Thirty minutes of sex can burn 144 calories. On the other hand, studies show that physical exercise in turn also enhances sexual performance.
9) Sex helps reduce and relieve pain. The oxytocin or "cuddling hormone" that makes couples want to snuggle and cuddle after sex dampens physical pain.
10) Sex brings happiness. Apart from oxytocin, sex releases serotine, endorphins, and phenylethylamine – hormones that bring feelings of euphoria, pleasure, and elation.
11) Sex helps both partners to sleep well. An orgasm brings with it a feeling of relaxation and comfort. The hormones produce and trigger the urge to cuddle or just "pass out".
12) It decreases risk of heart disease and stroke. Men with high libidos were seen to be less likely to suffer heart disease in studies done. This was because of their being more sexually active.
13) Frequent ejaculation in men is being said to help fight prostate cancer. Regular sex flushes out semen and any carcinogens lurking in the prostate gland. These carcinogens normally become cancerous.
14) During pregnancy, frequent sexual intercourse and exposure to semen can reduce the risk of developing a serious pregnancy complication called preeclampsia, which causes

swelling, headaches, and nausea. The protein in the semen helps regulate a woman's immune system.
15) Regular sex makes fertilization easier for those trying for kids. There is nothing like trying too much. An Australian Fertility center showed that men who ejaculated daily for seven days had high quality sperms at the end of the week, making it stronger to fertilize the female egg.
16) Regular sex in marriage takes away the temptation of adultery for both partners.
Take note of the second half of verse 5 in 1 Corinthians 7 vs 1-5.
(It is important to note that if one or both partners have a demon of lust or adultery no amount of marital sex can stop their adultery).
17) Sexual satisfaction in marriage generally causes both partners to have feelings of respect and goodwill towards each other.

This list may not be exhaustive, but I hope the message is clear – sex in marriage is good...no, it is great!

#SexIsAGiftFromGod

#RockMeTonightBabe

DR. TADIUS MAWOKO

CHAPTER 06

MONEY...HIS, HERS OR OURS?

Money, money, money! Money answers everything – Ecclesiastes 10 vs 19b.

Money is good! Yes, some religious people who think they are godly say money is evil. They even "quote" the Bible... in this case misquote it. Ecclesiastes 10 vs 19b says *"money answers everything."* The Bible does not say money is bad. 1 Timothy 6 vs 13 says – *"for the love of money is the root of all evil ..."* Check this out and note carefully – not money but the love of it is the root of ALL evil. So, money is good but our attitude towards it can be evil and dangerous. So, it is the love, the lust, the unbridled desire for money that is evil! God wants us to have money – LOTS OF IT!

Have you ever noticed that most of God servants in the bible were wealthy? Let us start with our father of faith, Father Abraham. In Genesis 24 vs 1 we are told, *"now Abraham was old, well advanced in age and the Lord had blessed him IN ALL THINGS"* (emphasis is mine).

Note well, ALL things! Money included. Genesis 13 vs 2 states, "Abraham was very rich in livestock, in SILVER, and in GOLD"! Hear that? Silver and Gold!

Isaac, his son, was so rich it intimidated the Philistines, and they evicted him from their land. Genesis 26 vs 13-16, *"The man (Isaac) began to prosper, and continued prospering until he became very prosperous for, he had possessions of flocks and possessions of herds and a great number of servants. So, the Philistines envied him. Now the Philistines had stopped up all the wells which his fathers' servants had dug in the days of Abraham his father and they had filled them with earth. And Abimelech said to Isaac, "Go away from us for you are much mightier than we.""* We know how Jacob got rich at Laban's place even after Laban had deceived him by giving him the wrong wife and changing the wages several times.

David was wealthy. His son Solomon is the richest man recorded in the bible.

We have New Testament men who were rich. Gaius – Paul's convert in Romans 16. Joseph of Arimathea whose special grave Jesus was buried in. Our Lord Jesus showed flashes of wealth himself.

Examples:
1) He allowed a thief, Judas Iscariot, to be the treasurer of His ministry – who stole from the coffers. Jesus, as God, knew Judas inside out, but still made him treasurer. The message here was – you can steal as much as you want, my ministry will not go broke.

2) Money out of fish! The first ever ATM! Even as God the son, he chose not to use his authority to dodge the temple tax but got money out of a fish to pay (Matthew 17v27).
3) When he died on the cross, his garment was fought for to such an extent that the Roman soldiers cast lots for it. Why would Roman soldiers, paid by the Roman Emperor, want the garment of a Jewish preacher? That is because it was special, unique, and expensive, we find the reference of this in the next few scriptures: Matthew 27 vs 35/ Mark 15 vs 24/ Luke 23 vs 34/ John 19 vs 24.

Jesus' clothes must have been pretty good to make it worthwhile for soldiers to cast lots for them.

So, money and wealth are good and are used to propagate the kingdom of God while the sinner will use the same to sin more and do abominable things. We come to realize that money and wealth simply take the character of who owns it. Money in the hands of a good man will bring good results, but money in the hand of an infidel or a weak believer becomes dangerous. Some people say when people become rich, they become proud. I beg to differ. Pride would already be in someone. Money simply brings it out. If you have no money – what can you be proud about? In the same vein, a humble man will stay humble even when he gets into tons of money. Now, as a Christian couple, desire for your money to mean something in the Kingdom of God. As believers, we must own our money – not the money to own us. We must control our money, not the money to control us. We must appreciate money and what it can be used for and not love it. A couple who loves money are the most pitiable people. You never get satisfied – you never live a life. You just gather and gather.

Here is a warning. The first sign of the love of money is not tithing. Do not be fooled, not tithing is the first sign of a lover of money. Tithe belongs to God. Not tithing is literally robbing God of His portion. Having the audacity to rob Him who gave you so much – your life, your spouse, the clothes on your back, the food you eat, the roof over your head (rental or owned), the car you drive and the fuel in it. It is about deciding to be godly and faithful. When you are faithful in little (tithe – 10%), God will make you Lord of much. If you cannot give a tithe of the $6000 you earn a month, why should God double your salary to $12 000? Now, your education (which God gave you), can sometimes cause you to be promoted and other factors too and you will earn $12 000, but its buying power in your life will be $6 000 or less because God is not in it.

God has a blueprint for our lives including our wealth. He wants us to prosper like Abraham. That's why he engrafted us into the commonwealth of Israel (Romans 11 v 11-31). We are Israel by faith. Abraham is our father – like father like son! But it is of little value to sing the song: "Abraham's blessings are mine", when we are not doing what Abraham did. Like father like son in doing – and then like father like son in the reaping. In Genesis 14 vs 19-20 Abraham gave his tithe. If Abraham's blessings are mine – then tithing is mine as well.

Kingdom couples live by kingdom principles and laws. You cannot be in USA and try to live by the rules and laws of another country. In God's Kingdom, you run finances God's way to prosper. Remember that all wealth and all power to get wealth comes from Him. (Deuteronomy 8v18). God gives you power to get (birth) wealth.

A Kingdom couple must tithe and give to God while running their finances the Kingdom way. Give to relatives and friends when they are in need. A couple must be generous. The rule of thumb for money is you spend some, you give some, and you save some. A wise couple invests both spiritually and physically. Investing spiritually is tithing, giving for the work of God, and giving to the needy. Physical investment is through savings, stock, shares, other market investments and business. Get shares, stocks, real estate, and other investments. You may decide to get an investment advisor to help you.

#MoneyAnswersAllThings

CHAPTER 07

DEALING WITH IN-LAWS

The legendary and proverbial fight between mothers-in-law and daughters-in-law or sons-in-law is unfortunately real in many families. There can even be fights between sisters-in-law, that is – the new bride and the husband's sisters. The silliest one is the fight between sisters-in-law as wives of brothers.

Many jokes have been coined about these 'in-law wars'. Name calling has been prevalent as well. I know of a man who called his mother-in-law "the dragon lady", another called his mother-in-law "the witch" – I am serious! Name calling between mothers and daughters-in-law is common in many circumstances. Some men live all their lives realizing that there is a continual war without a truce between their mothers and their wives. I will share a joke I heard years ago, even before I got married myself. A mother sends her latest picture to her son and daughter-in-law. The mail arrives while the son is at work and the wife (daughter-in-law) is at home. The daughter-in-law opens the mail and finds her mother-in-law's picture. The husband arrives home and sees the wife in the toilet with his mother's picture. The man asks, "What are you doing in the toilet with my mom's picture?" The wife answers, "It just arrived today, and I am looking for the most suitable place for it in here!"

There are a lot of dynamics that come to play in the in-law relationships. Some problems emanate from words spoken or misspoken even before the wedding. Others from sheer misunderstandings. Most mother and daughter-in-law fights originate from the fact that they love the same man! The mother loves her son and is possessive, or thinks the wife is not good enough or worthy of her son. The wife sees her mother-in-law to be possessive, nosy, and intrusive and unable to cut the umbilical cord and let the son go. There is a great possibility that barring the grace of God, such a relationship can be unto death and the poor man has to be the umpire and peace maker between the two women in his life whom he loves and cherishes! What a task!

In the early years of my marriage, I had to do this – play umpire. But thank God my wife found grace to work this out and convince my dear mother that they were friends not foes and that I, as the common man in their lives had enough love for both – different types of love of course! Gwen showered my mom with love and providence that there was a "cease fire" that was permanent. My mom and wife became such great friends that when my mother suffered senile dementia, she quickly forgot my face, and she could not recognize my face but for a very long time but continued to recognize her daughter-in-love (my wife) and would heartily greet her repeatedly in a space of a few hours. Poor me was forgotten and always had to introduce and reintroduce myself several times in the space of a few hours. Gwen absolutely enjoyed this, and I was playfully jealous about it. How can a mother forget the face of her son but pleasantly remember the face of his wife?

With a little help from me, Gwen had managed to win my mother's heart. She had managed to let my mother see her as a daughter and friend and not as the rival who had come to snatch her beloved son and breadwinner away from her. In fact, my wife and my sisters' relationships are so good that whenever my wife is not happy about me, I get into trouble from one particular sister. Most of it is petty though, but it always happens that if she asks for something I consider unimportant and I say "no" to her, she waits until one of my sisters is around and Gwen starts the issue again knowing she always has my sister's support and so she wins!

My spiritual father Apostle Dr. E.H Guti says that the rivalry and fight between mother-in-law and daughter-in-law is probably that these are the two women who have seen this man completely naked! The mother bathed him and took care of him in the nude – now the wife is also seeing him in the nude in the bedroom! Interesting point to ponder on! Bad in-law relationships are also found in the bible.

There is a verse in Genesis that has caused my wife to pray for the right wife for our eldest child (our son), and the right husbands for our two daughters. She started praying for spouses for our children when our son was in his early teens and the daughters were still pre-teens.

Here are the verses that when my wife read, she jumped into action and has prayed about this ever since:

Genesis 26:34-35 - *"When Esau was forty years old, he took as wives Judith the daughter of Beeri the Hittite and Basemath the daughter of Elon the Hittite. And they were a grief of mind to Isaac and Rebekah".*

You see, Esau's two wives from an unbelieving and uncircumcised nation became a source of grief to Isaac and Rebekah. We pray it will not be like this for us. What were Judith and Basemath doing that grieved their father and mother-in-law so much that it had to be recorded in scripture? It seems in this case, that Esau was on a mission to inflict pain on his parents for his losing the birthright to Jacob. Check this one out Genesis 28 vs 6-9 - "Esau saw that Isaac had blessed Jacob and sent him away to Padam Aram to take himself a wife from there and that as he blessed him, he gave him a charge saying "You shall not take a wife from the daughters of Canaan and that Jacob had obeyed his father and his mother and had gone to Padan Aram. Also, Esau saw that the daughters of Canaan did not please his father, Isaac. So, Esau went and took Mahaketh the daughter of Ishmael, Abraham's son, the sister of Nebajoth, to be his wife in addition to the wives he had". This is when the modern generation exclaim, "Really?" If Esau wanted to make amends why not go to Padan Aram there and take another wife from his mother's kinsmen?

Most in-law fights are like this:
   a) daughter-in-law vs mother-in-law.
   b) son-in-law vs mother-in-law.
   c) daughter-in-law vs sister-in-law (husband's sister).
   d) daughter-in-law vs sister-in-law (husband's brother's wife).
   e) daughter-in-law vs brother-in-law (husband's brother).
   f) son-in-law vs father-in-law.
   g) daughter-in-law vs father-in-law.

The last three are the least common but are not non-existent.

Let us try and see what normally causes all these problems as we follow the relationships above with the statement below corresponding to each item above.

a)
  i. Failure to share the man (son/husband).
  ii. Mother failing to let go, in other words, failing to cut the umbilical cord and allow her son to enjoy his wife and new life.
  iii. Mother failing to come to terms with the fact that her son now loves another woman apart from her.
  iv. Daughter-in-law coming into the family on a high horse and disrespecting her mother-in-law (or other members of the family).
  v. Daughter-in-law disrupting the traditions and customs of this family with new demands or refusal to be part of the family at large.
  vi. Daughter-in-law's wrong sense of possessiveness – she wants to "own" the man completely and cut all ties.
  vii. Daughter-in-law influencing her husband to stop supporting his parents or family members financially and other ways.
  viii. Foul mouth of mother-in-law of which the bride hears of it and decides to "punish" her mother-in-law for her foul words.
  ix. Bride running off her mouth about things she is not familiar with in her groom's family.
  x. Unforgiveness from either or both sides.

b)
  i. Mother-in-law thinking her son-in-law is not good enough or wealthy enough to marry her daughter.
  ii. Mother-in-law being nosy and wants to control her son-in-law's decisions.

YOUR MARRIAGE… HEAVEN OR HELL ON EARTH?

    iii.   Mother-in-law influencing her daughter negatively and causing her to rebel against the husband and not submit.
    iv.   Son-in-law disrespecting his mother-in-law.
    v.   Son-in-law cutting off all help his wife was giving to parents before marriage.

c)
    i.   Husband's sister is jealous that her big brother or young brother's heart has been taken by another woman. The sister starts getting insecure, assuming that her brother will love her less now that he has a wife in his life.
    ii.   Husband's sister's notion that her sister-in-law is not looking after her brother well enough.
    iii.   Daughter-in-law wants husband to cut off help of any kind to his sister.
    iv.   Husband's sister thinks that with his wife on the scene, her brother will not be as available to help or support her.

d)
    i.   New daughter-in-law comes on a high horse and disrupts the peace of the sister-in-law married earlier into the family by another brother.
    ii.   Older daughter-in-law cannot stand her new sister-in-law because the new sister-in-law now gets all the family attention and this makes her feel like an old shoe (she may have been a star daughter-in-law which changed when the new one with probably more beauty, more poise, more class, more education, better background came into the picture).
    iii.   Good old rivalry from both sides, and this can even separate brothers or at least create mistrust and drifting apart.

e)

i. Husband's brother dislikes new sister-in-law because she has destroyed "the boys club." He cannot hang out with his brother as often as before.
   ii. Financial help from his brother is now in doubt now that he has "another expense" and new plans.
   iii. New daughter/ sister-in-law does not want hubby to be hanging around his brother anymore, she needs his attention.
   iv. Brother thinks his new sister-in-law is not respecting the family (in whichever context he chooses to put it in).

f)
   i. Father-in-law, like most men, thinks his son-in-law is not good enough or wealthy enough to marry his princess and can even voice it. (Apparently this is the biggest problem between father-in-law and son-in-law).
   ii. Father-in-law wants to dominate his son-in-law and rule his home.
   iii. Father-in-law can be too demanding or too judgmental.
   iv. Son-in-law simply disrespects his father-in-law (or father-in-law perceives so).
   v. Father-in-law perceives (even wrongly) that his daughter is being ill-treated.

g)
   i. Father-in-law simply does not think his daughter-in-law is good enough for his golden boy.
   ii. The daughter-in-law thinks the father-in-law is a bad influence on her husband.
   iii. Daughter-in-law detests the fact that her father-in-law wants his son to run his new family exactly the way he (the father)

ran his family (even when circumstances, times and other factors are different) and there are signs of some failures in that family the husband comes from.

The problems mentioned above are real. Many a time, my wife and I have counseled couples that have the above issues. It is obvious that the enemy of God, the enemy of God's creation and enemy of marriages – the devil, instigates and promotes the above problems. These problems are so prevalent, even among Christian families. Many daughters and sons-in-law talk about their mothers-in-law as "MONSTERS-in-law". This should not be. In-laws should work out issues. According to God, relationships in families are meant to be sweet. Mothers-in-law should come to a place they call their new daughters "daughters-in-love", and the daughters-in-law/ love must come to love their mother-in-law such that they call them "mothers-in-love". Indeed, it is because of the love between sons and daughters of man that results in marriage and into bringing of families together.

There are ways relationships can be healed or this disaster can be avoided from the onset – even from the very time of dating. Here are some suggestions that have worked:

1. Exchange parents – Yes, exchange families. Husband should endeavor to look after and help his wife's parents and family and vice versa. In this case the wife must educate her family that when they need anything they must not contact her but their new son – because that is what he is – an adopted son by marriage. In the same vein, the husband must train his 'people' that their 'new daughter' now has responsibility over them and if they need help they must contact her. This kills the selfishness where one spouse keeps doing good things for the family he/she comes from and abandons the new

family he/she is married into. If the other spouse tends to forget or to act slowly, it is the duty of the other spouse to remind him/her gently. This has worked wonders in many families including mine.

2. Compete in doing good – to each other and each other's family. Try and outdo your spouse in doing good, not in-laws.
3. Shield your spouse – from bad actions and words your relative may say or do to him/her. Do not repeat them to him/her – you destroy relationships. Additionally, do not allow your family to talk negatively about your spouse. Fight for each other and for your marriage.
4. Desist as much as possible from reporting every argument about your misunderstandings – Go to neutral people to counsel you e.g., pastors and elders or professional counselors. Never tell your family of your spouse's wrongdoing and failures. Your family will hate him/her and even when you two resolve your issues and kiss and make up and are happy – your relatives still think you are married to a "terrorist". Even when it is you who was wrong – they usually take your side because blood is thicker than water.
5. Exercise love – 1 Peter 4 vs 8 states: "Above all, love one another deeply because love covers a multitude of sins." When you love someone, you ignore some of their mistakes and those you fail to ignore, you quickly forgive because that is simply what love does.
6. Study your new family – Even when you are still dating, study your future spouse's family. Know what you are getting into. To be forewarned is to be forearmed. Think of how to sidestep each argument, each potential trap from the devil through your in-laws. Know the crazy ones in your spouse's family and avoid them as much as you can.

7. Be united as a couple – Always display a united front. Even if your spouse is in error, cover him/her and solve and correct each other privately. If you correct your spouse in the presence of your family, they take this as a license to attack him/her. They will say you agree that your spouse is not good.
8. Appreciate your in-laws – no matter how flawed they are! They raised that handsome man you call "hubby". They sacrificed a lot to raise that cute girl you call "babe", "honey", or "bae"! No one is perfect. Be thankful for the fact that the family provided you with a spouse. Learn to appreciate all your in-laws.
9. Sh-h-h-shut your mouth – this is the title of one of my favorite books from my spiritual father, the late Apostle E.H Guti. Talking too much, fuming on your mouth, chattering on like a radio station will get you into trouble. You will be bound to say the wrong things that will cause your in-laws to hate you. Do not give them that chance. Zip it! Yes-zip it!

Most people you talk to can give you the impression that a good relationship with in-laws is not possible! This is the devil's lie. To conclude this chapter, I want to bring your attention to an often-quoted scripture from Ruth 1 vs 16b, *"... for wherever you go I will go, and wherever you lodge I will lodge, your people shall be my people and your God shall be my God."* Now, you have often heard these vows of love between a bride and groom at weddings – yet, as you see in this verse, this was not between a husband and wife. This was said by Ruth, a daughter-in-law to Naomi, her mother-in-law. So, these beautiful, sweet words we hear repeatedly at weddings were not originally said at a marriage ceremony but at a crucial time when a mother-in-law was releasing her daughters-in-law and one of them, who loved her so much, would not leave her. Ruth said these words. My sister, my brother, in-laws can be loved in spite of disagreements!

#MotherInloveNotMonsterInLaw

CHAPTER

08

OTHER PROBLEMS IN MARRIAGE

Communication, sex, money and dealing with in-laws are definitely the biggest and most problematic of all marriage woes – but they are definitely not the only problems a couple can face in marriage. People's backgrounds, temperaments and character flaws all have an effect on marriage.

Let us start with the background. In our time, every parent would always be interested in knowing the background of the family their daughter or son was marrying into. They knew very well that the circumstances or situations a person grows up in will be reenacted. For example, a girl who grew up in a family where loud voices and screaming were part and parcel of everyday conversation, believes it to be normal and will shout and scream when she gets married. If she saw her mother bullying and overruling her father, she thinks it is normal and carries it into her marriage where she will certainly meet tough resistance and opposition, leading to fights. On the other hand, a young man who grows up seeing his dad dominate his mother and the whole family, may think that abuse is part and parcel of the game and in turn be abusive. It is clear that background does influence a marriage positively or negatively depending on how these spouses were brought up and what they experienced. Wrong things become normal to them in marriage because they grew up in them and did not know anything better. Temperaments are another factor. If a couple's temperaments are not checked deliberately by the couple, they can always end up in fights. We will talk about these temperaments and personalities in a later chapter.

Character … character … character! This is one thing we cannot hide forever. So, during courtship, both parties are trying to put their best foot forward (individually) – and make the best impression ever. After the honeymoon, or even during the honeymoon, true character starts coming out – it cannot be hidden forever. A lousy character will remain a pain in the neck for one particular spouse and vice versa.

Examples of some bad characteristics are:
a) Someone who never apologizes no matter how wrong they are.
b) A spouse who is quick to pick up an argument even where it was not supposed to be.
c) A messy spouse, with dirty clothes everywhere, and dishes done once a week etc.
d) Spending too much time on social media while the spouse cries for attention.
e) Violence – a character that is physically violent by nature.
f) Laziness – a man or woman who cannot pin down a job – they simply do not like work.

YOUR MARRIAGE… HEAVEN OR HELL ON EARTH?

> g) Unappreciation – someone cannot appreciate when a spouse or anyone does something for them.
> h) Demanding – no matter what the spouse does, it is not enough. This is sick! They want you to kiss the ground they walk on.
> i) Lack of boundaries – they do or say things anytime, anyplace, to anyone.
> j) Lack of discretion – and it embarrasses the spouse until it kills his//her love.

We all know that we all are not angels and each one of us has a character flaw. The ideal is to hear from others including your spouse and make a determined decision to change. As we do that, God's grace kicks in and we get victory and improve ourselves and our marriages bit by bit.

Other problems are caused by the birth order. Birth order is the position or number an individual is born among his/her siblings in the family. We have first-borns, middle children and the last-born. These three groups behave very differently. First-borns are goal getters, strict, ambitious and want all people to be in line. They can be perfectionists too! They want to lead. Middle children in general are peacemakers and can be withdrawn as they are used to being outshone by the first-born and the attention grabber last-born. Middle children can be rebellious to prove that they do exist because attention is mostly given to the first and last born.

On the other hand, the last-born in most families is the clown of the family – the joker. They normally get away with murder much to the chagrin of the rest. Most last-borns continue to take themselves as the baby of the family and so expect everyone to run around for them and to help them in every way. They get spoiled and they can be irresponsible with money. All these characteristics of the siblings can affect their marriages. Can you imagine two first- born individuals being married? Both want to lead. The two last-borns together in marriage can live in debt if not counseled. The characteristic of middle and last-borns can differ from the norm depending on how big the gap is with the older siblings.

#DetermineToChangeBadCharacter

CHAPTER 09

GROOMING AND MINISTERING TO EACH OTHER

Real marriage is never for the selfish. If any of the two in a marriage is selfish, that marriage will experience numerous difficulties. The fact that the Word (the Bible) says "the two shall be one" makes it clear that it is no longer me, me, me but us! Therefore, a couple must try to outdo one another in doing good. Outdo each other in serving. Outdo each other in loving. Outdo each other in giving. Outdo each other in putting the other spouse first in all things. Outdo each other in satisfying one another in bed. The spirit of me, myself, I must die.

John 12 vs 24 says, *"Most assuredly, I say to you, unless a grain of wheat falls to the ground and dies, it remains alone, but if it dies, it produces much grain"*.

A husband or a wife must die to self - we call this the dying seed principle. No seed can germinate and reproduce and be productive unless and until it dies. So, a man or woman ought to die to self to produce. Both partners will produce a lot when they die to self, since marriage is about sharing. Marriage is about giving and receiving; you cannot always receive without giving. It has been said before, there are those who love the idea of being married but are not prepared to labor at it to make it work. It is never automatic. A real man must cultivate his wife because each wife is raw material with unfathomable potential. When God gives a woman to a man, he has entrusted that man to unlock the potential in that woman and vice versa. The woman of Proverbs 31 did not just happen to be there but must have been supported by her husband. The old adage "behind every successful man is a great woman" is not a cliché. When we groom and support each other, we always manage to build a strong marriage.

1 Corinthians 11 vs 7b *"...the woman is the glory of man."* Many Christian articles have been written about this scripture and some of them may seem sexist. However, my understanding is that a woman adds glory to a man she is married to. In the same vein that it is not good for a man to be alone, and a helpmate fit for him was created – that helper makes a man shine more in society. Take proverbs 31 vs 23 for example, *"Her husband is known in the gates when he sits among the elders of the land."* Let us understand this scripture in its cultural context. In those days, approved (and esteemed) men would sit by the gates of a city where they would solve the problems of the city and bring justice when there were arguments between individuals. So those who sat at the gate were esteemed, mature men of the city, esteemed rulers – justice brokers, before a case was elevated to the King! Now the husband of the Proverbs 31 virtuous woman is well known at the gates. He is obviously a wiseman, but his "celebrity status" is not because of his wisdom but according to

the context of this scripture – he is well known because of the outstanding woman. Thus, she has become the glory of her husband.

That said, the husband must therefore polish this "diamond" that gives him glory and continue to polish it to shine more and more. If, as a man you marry a wife without a college degree, if she so desires it is your duty to financially and morally support her to get that degree. If she has an undergraduate degree and desires a masters – support her, if she wants to go for a PhD, support her! If your wife wants to be a businesswoman, by all means, support her.
I must emphasize this because in the communities I have been, I have noticed women who break their backs working to support a husband who would be studying. The husband goes on to take a Bachelors, a Masters, and even a PhD while the wife pays some of the tuition fees or at least is paying rent, buying food, paying utilities, and clothing the children. You would then think that now that the husband has his desired Masters or PhD he will give a chance to his wife who is also desiring to advance in education – but alas – no! He tells her that his brother or his sister needs to go to university too and expects the wife to play second fiddle to his brother or sister. Surely, some men have no clue! When your wife has slaved for you to accomplish your academic dream – now it is her turn to fulfil her academic goals, but you will not support her but bring in your brother or sister onto the scene? How selfish is that? This normally happens in African communities in the diaspora. A wise man grooms his wife in every manner. In his marriage book called "Sh-h-h Shut your mouth" Dr. Ezekiel H. Guti says, "The husband must work out his wife until she is a good wife because that woman is his garden to till. Every woman needs a husband who is strong. When God created Adam, he gave him work to till and to look after the garden" (P.34- 2006 Edition). In Genesis 2 vs 15, "God

placed man in the garden of Eden to tend it and watch over it". This is God training a man in the art of tending (cultivating) nurturing – before He gave man a wife. The Hebrew word for "tend" means "to foster growth, to improve by labor, care or study, to refine".

So, a husband should:
1) Cause his wife to grow (in every manner).
2) Improve her (in every area) with labor, care, study, and to refine her.

It is the responsibility of every man to foster and enhance growth and improve his wife. As the Hebrew word suggests "with labor", it indicates that it is not easy. Some wives do not realize that though you love them, they may have a lot to improve on. They may perceive it as you saying they are useless, or that somebody's wife is better than them. So, you use wisdom and choose your words carefully as a husband. Do it with care, cause her to desire it – to love to achieve. The part of "study" means study your wife and know how to handle her. Women are more dynamic than men. Even if she chooses a degree, she may change courses three times before she settles on a particular course or degree. Patience is required. As a man, you chose your wife because you thought "she is so fine" yet she still can be refined.

Now to the woman, allow your husband to cultivate you. Allow him to improve you and refine you. Why settle for what you have or what you are already when you can have more or be better academically, socially, spiritually, and physically. As a pastor and counselor, I have had to struggle with women who are lazy or proud or simply ignorant – whose husbands want the best for them but they themselves are oblivious to this fact. Every man wants a woman he can be proud of. He was proud of you when you married, but times and situations change. He wants to move with the times and so should you. Listen to your husband, my sister. When he suggests these things, he wants the best of you and the best from you. You will reap the rewards if you listen and cooperate. He will love you more, appreciate you more and honor you more and value you more.

Remember, every man has an ego. That ego drives him to thrive to be the best in providing, best in making love, best raising children, best in dressing his wife and making her look like a queen. He wants you to look the most gorgeous at a party, wedding or at church. He wants to feel attracted to you all the days of his life, both intellectually and physically. And spiritually too! Intellectually, he needs to have an intelligent conversation with you. Stop being "clueless", sister! Physically he wants you to look a million bucks in body or dressing. Spiritually he desires you to bring the house down when you preach and be effective in the house of God. He simply desires you to be "the head and not the tail" so do not resist his cultivation. My sister, improve your education if your husband is asking you to. And you must create a desire for it for yourself not to just do it "for him". Improve your body – eat less /eat well, exercise. Many women have too many useless excuses on this. Keep healthy and attractive. Know what type of dressing is best for you. Not everything in fashion is for you.

Wear what agrees with your body shape – beautiful, but modest and classy. It does not have to be expensive either. It is about color coordination, fitting and presentation. If he wants you to accompany him for a jog, walk or to the gym, go with him. Why should he be seeing those beautiful firm bodies at the gym when you can be like that too? Allow hubby to groom you and to minister to you.

A good husband ministers to his wife. When was the last time you massaged her feet or shoulders or whole body? When was the last time you made her a cup of coffee or tea? When was the last time you did the dishes or vacuumed the carpet? Taking out trash to the bin, and the bin to the kerb for collection is your duty, brother – not hers. Filling up the gas tank on all your vehicles is your duty, brother not hers. Getting the cars to the service shop is our duty as men, not for the ladies. In other words, I am saying "treat her like a lady!" Buy her perfume. Let her smell good. Buy her lingerie. It is a marital crime for a husband to pull down the pants of his wife when he does not know who bought them. You either go and buy the pants and bras for her on your own (you must know the sizes) or with her. You can also specifically give her money for pants and bras – not for her to take from the grocery money. When you give her the money for lingerie she should come and show you what she bought – she can even model for you in her new lingerie.

I know some men are even shocked when I say buy lingerie for my wife. Yes, the two shall be one. I love it when I go into a lingerie shop and buy items for my wife. The ladies there cast funny looks at me and I enjoy it. When they help me around the store or assist me at the checkout counter, they enquire who it is for. They say, "Who is the lucky lady?" They usually think it is for a girlfriend or mistress. I enjoy the look on their faces even more when I say it is for my wife. Then suddenly they assume that we are newlyweds and mention that. Imagine their further surprise when I tell them that my wife and I have been married for over thirty-five years!
Many husbands do not know the sizes of the bras and undies of their wives. I usually joke with men saying they know the boot (trunk) size of their cars but do not know the "boot" size of their wives. When you want to load speakers or other PA equipment in their car boot, they

will just look and tell you accurately whether it fits or not. But not with their wives' "boot". But do not buy her undies that look like a World War II German parachute, or the feet of a duck. Look for something modern, sexy but comfortable.

As a wife, you must also groom your husband. It is your duty to see that he looks good among other men. I see married men wearing jackets that are too big or the sleeves too long. Others also wear trousers that are too long, and they are literally stepping on the trousers as they walk. Where is the wife? Other men's dressing is so uncoordinated even if the clothes are good quality. Many men do not know how to dress properly. You see a grown-up married man appearing in public looking like a decorated Christmas tree. Where is the wife? Where was she when he walked out of the house? It is even worse when they go out together and she is by his side, all-smiling, with her husband looking like that. Surely, a caring wife could have coordinated her husband's dressing at home! Some husbands need training too in how to dress and how to groom themselves. Remember,1 Corinthians 7 vs 4 says a spouse does not have authority over their body but their partner does. This is about sex, but also applies to clothes, or grooming. I want my wife to dress a certain way and she likes me to dress in a certain way too. Many a times I have been made to change clothes after dressing to go out even to the shops for a few groceries because my wife was not happy with what I was wearing. Many times, she has asked me to change my clothes even at my house because some people were coming over to visit. In Dallas TX, USA, she made me shave off all my beard as soon as I entered the house from the barber because she did not like my new beard style with sideburns. I was disappointed she did not like my "new look", but I did not complain – it is her body – her face that she kisses. A good wife serves her husband food whenever she is able, not just say every day, "Take your food from the oven." A good wife notices when her hubby has had a tough day at work and helps him settle down. She can also massage him just like he massages her as mentioned earlier in this chapter. It is good to do unto others as you would like them to do unto you.

Wives – help us husbands even with cleanliness. A man is normally not fazed to wear a shirt three times before it is washed. Some even repeat underwear! A wife is there to say "no" to that! Wife, help him to choose a good deodorant or cologne that makes him smell good – the way you like him to smell. Do you serve him tea or coffee like I have also asked the man to serve you? As a wife, encourage your husband to develop himself. Do not nag him. Do not force him. Do not compare him with his friends or brethren at church. Do not tell him which course to take, simply suggest with a sweet spirit. His development increases his earning power and boosts his confidence. There are times when you must give him sex when you are not in the mood because your body is his according to scripture, and you will be ministering or serving your husband and vice versa, when it is the wife who needs to be served.

A good wife encourages her husband to excel. She speaks to him words of affirmation. This is the love language of many people, especially men. Vocalize their achievements and celebrate their victories. Husbands ought to do the same with their wives. Try and at least tolerate your husband's favorite sport and watch it together with him. As much as you love "hubby" to go shopping with you and watch some of those romantic comedies he does not care about. Watch with him as his favorite soccer team win or lose. (WARNING! Do not say too much when his team loses).

YOUR MARRIAGE... HEAVEN OR HELL ON EARTH?

When all is said and done, a couple must work at improving, grooming, and serving each other the rest of their lives

#KnowHerBootSize

CHAPTER

10

INVESTING IN YOUR MARRIAGE
(You can't withdraw where you DIDN'T deposit or invest)

This chapter goes hand in hand with the previous one (Chapter 9) on serving and grooming each other. We must appreciate that marriage is a living organism and as such must be fed to survive and thrive. The type of "food" a couple feed their marriage will correspond with results they will get in their marriage. Positive "food" results in a happy thriving marriage while negative "food" results in an unhealthy marriage, which, if nothing is changed, that marriage dies sooner or later.

Marriage is also like a bank account or an investment. It means we need to deposit individually or together as a couple. In marriage there will be demands and needs we will ask of each other, simply because by being married, we are expected to cater to each other's needs as spouses. There are times we must "withdraw" from this account called marriage. But if we make several withdrawals without depositing anything our "marriage account" soon becomes empty and bankrupt. We are all aware that having a bank card and the pin is not an assurance that you can go and withdraw money at the ATM. There MUST be money in the account for us to get some at the ATM. If there is nothing in the account, we just get a slip from the ATM written "insufficient funds!" There are people who withdraw and withdraw from their marriages without depositing anything. One partner or both may be guilty of this.

So, what do we do as a couple? It is a no brainer that we must invest in our marriage every chance we get so we do not go "bankrupt". What does this mean – you may ask! Well, let us do things in our marriages that enhance our marriages. Here are some things we can do. Note – this is not exhaustive list:

1. Attend couples' seminars and retreats.
    You do not attend them because things are bad in your marriage, but you attend them to:
    a) service and "change oil" in a marriage.
    b) simply refresh your marriage.
    c) get group counseling together with others before things go bad.
    d) get to know areas that need improvement.
    e) learn from other couples.

2. Buy and read good books on marriage.
    No one is born with knowledge to run a marriage, but we can learn from gifted authors. Reading the Word of God and different books on marriage will surely add value to a marriage.

3. Take holidays.

Getting away from the same old familiar four walls as a couple does wonders. It is of paramount importance for a couple to be able to "escape", detox and refocus. Every time Gwen and I go for even a few days' rest, we find time to discuss our marriage without any pressure that may cause a spark of "negative fire" that would probably happen if we tackled some issues under pressure at home. Holidays are an essential therapy. It is you and your babe without the worry of cooking, dishes, cleaning, and the busy schedule.

4. Date night.

    Date nights are always a pressure valve that releases pressure regularly before you can take that vacation. Your romance is rejuvenated during date nights. You can even dress up in a tuxedo and frock, just for the two of you.

5. Buy each other gifts.

    Gifts mean a lot to some people, especially to our wives. They do not have to be expensive all the time but thoughtful, funny, and romantic. Perfumes, lingerie, and chocolates usually win hands down.

6. Counseling.

    A couple does not have to wait until things are not right to get counseling. A couple must get regular counseling even informally. By this I mean going to your counselors when you do not have questions to ask them but just talking to them as a couple. Usually, God drops something to help you guard against complacency and get wisdom in general.

YOUR MARRIAGE… HEAVEN OR HELL ON EARTH?

Yes, most of the above need money – but that is why it is an investment! You do not deposit air but something tangible. But if you think paying for couples' retreat and holidays takes a lot of your money, try a divorce lawyer! Lawyers wipe you out and you are left cashless and spouseless. Even simple things like men saying "yes" to shopping is a great investment. We will reap the results soon enough for this sacrificial investment.

So, what are you waiting for? Plan and commit to attend that next couples' retreat or take that holiday. Invest, the withdrawal is always sweet! Kind words and vocalizing compliments and appreciation are an investment.

Withdrawals are those times of pressure, testing and marital expectations or married life demands that just come. They leave us unscathed because we would be running deep in our stability and patience for one another.

#HolidayThings

CHAPTER 11

ADVICE TO MEN – LOVE HER

Ephesians 5 vs 25 states: *"Husbands, love your wives just as Christ loved the church and gave Himself up for her."*

The above scripture is indeed a tall order, but it is not a suggestion – it is a commandment. Every husband is commanded to love his own wife, just like every wife is commanded to submit to her own husband. This is a perfect godly balance. It is hard for a woman to submit to a brute that does not love her. It is also hard for a man to continue to love a wife who does not submit. However hard it is, it is not negotiable. A husband can love a wife into submission. When you demonstrate love to her, you can guide her to the right paths of submission and respect. Some men say how can I love a wife who does not respect me? Well, Christ's love for his church has been unconditional and He expects us to do likewise. It is not always that the church is obedient to Christ - it sometimes gets to stray away here and there due to politics, and popular doctrine that might not be hundred percent from God. Yet Jesus brings the church back into his arms and washes it by His Word. (Ephesians 5 vs 26).

It is also important to note that the above scripture does not stand alone. Colossians 3 vs 19 says, *"Husbands love your wives and do not be bitter towards them"*. There are times when men are bitter towards their wives due to many reasons. The major one is when the wife is stingy with sex, then other reasons like overspending, disrespect, not loving his relatives – especially his mother, bad words coming out of her mouth and sometimes the devastating issue of her flirting with other men to say the least, come to the fore. But the commandment stands – love her! I told you it is a tall order but that is the commandment from God.

Not only that, but Ephesians Chapter 5 vs 29 says, *"So husbands ought to love their own wives as their own bodies; he who loves his wife loves himself"*. The husband and wife are one flesh. A few scriptures to support this come from Genesis 2 vs 24, Ephesians 5 vs 31, Matthew 19 vs 5, Mark 10 vs 7, 1 Corinthians 6 vs1b. So, she is you and you are her – you two are one. So, hating her is hating yourself. Not loving her is not loving yourself. Being bitter towards her is being bitter towards yourself. Nobody ever said it was going to be easy.

Here are eight (8) ways to love your wife which I got from a study online on this subject of loving wife:

1. Love her Heart – Emotional Love.
    Use words like "honey", "my love", "babe", "sweetie" etc. The Song of Solomon is full of words like "my love", "my dove",

"my fair lover". It is hard for any woman to resist a husband who speaks to her like this. Tell her you love her every day.

2. Love Her Mind – Intellectual Love.
   Convince your wife that she is the most important person in your life. Let her know you treasure her advice, thoughts, and suggestions. Tell her she is valuable to you and what she thinks and says is important to you. Engage her mind like you won her hand in marriage by engaging her in conversation, maintain it this way in marriage.

3. Love Her Body – Physical Love.
   Strive to satisfy your wife sexually. 1 Corinthians 7 vs 3, 5, 33. Touch her, kiss her, embrace her, show her affection in public. Tell her she is beautiful. She may not have the body of Miss Universe, but she is yours. If you will never get your wife to orgasm in bed you are lacking as a husband. She must get pleasure. She is your world. Compliment her body. Read Song of Solomon if you have no idea how to do it. No part of her body is out of bounds for your compliments. Tell her how her body turns you on.

4. Love Her Soul – Spiritual Love.
   Men often neglect this responsibility – the cultivation of godliness in our wives. Joshua 24 vs 14 to 15 says, *"As for me and my house, we will serve the Lord"*. It is a man's God-given responsibility to lead and cause your family – more so your wife, to worship God and to grow. We are the heads. Some decisions may not be popular with her, but you need to make them. Tell her we are going to church even though the Elder's wife hurt you last Sunday! Or we are going to church

even though for some reason you do not feel like it. There are a few times I have dragged myself out of bed to go to church and so I understand. Also, there are those days I have dragged my wife to church. Yes, we are both pastors, but it is not every Sunday we "feel" like going to church. It is about discipline and our love for God. We give ourselves as a living sacrifice. There are days when my wife jokingly says, "I wouldn't have come to church if it wasn't for the fact that I live at the pastor's house." It makes me crack up in laughter. I love her soul too much to let it gather moss and coldness at home when others are praising God at church. Check on her prayer life and study of the word as well. Let her prosper spiritually.

5. Love Her Relationships – Relational Love.
Love her relatives especially those she expresses more love towards. Love her friends and help her focus on those friends that are best for her – those that bring out the best of her. Protect her from your relatives and from her relatives. Protect her from your children. Do not allow your children to disrespect their mum. I have had to strongly discipline my three children at different times they acted untowardly towards my wife – or spoke rudely. I have long established this and they know that she may be their mom - but she is MY WIFE! Also stop contradicting her in front of the children or in a crowd.

6. Love Her Humanity – Realistic love.
No wife is perfect, so she is bound to make mistakes and disappoint you. But we men are not perfect either! So, when she blunders, which she will, be gracious to her. Love her

despite her human failures, she is human - like you. She may hurt you – but love her still. Forgive her and move on. 1 Peter 4 vs 8 says, "And above all things have fervent love for one another, for love will cover a multitude of sins".

7. Love Her Calling – Supportive Love.
   Part of a woman's duty and calling is to be submissive to her own husband. So, a loving husband helps his wife to be submissive by making it easy for her to submit. As a man, submit to all authority (Romans 13 vs 1) and this becomes an example to your wife. You cannot rebel against the church council, badmouth the Pastor, complain about your boss always, speak badly about the government and civil authorities and expect her to submit to you. As a husband, submit to your head – Jesus Christ (1 Corinthians 11 vs 3) and to all authority Romans 13 vs 1 and your wife will have a good model to emulate and copy from. Also, see where your wife's ministry calling is at church and support her. Find her calling also in society and allow her to do her civic duties with freedom and encouragement from you. She may be called to be a great businesswoman, love her calling and support her completely. Does she love writing? Encourage her to write books. Does she love helping other women in marriage? Love it and urge her on. Love her calling. Do not be jealous of her abilities, gifts and calling.

8. Love Her Maker – Theological Love.
   Some men struggle in really loving people and even their wives particularly because their love for God is not much. When we love God, He spreads His love in us, and we can love others – even our wives. God empowers us to love our

wives when we draw nearer to Him. Galatians 2 vs 2b says, *"Who loved me and gave Himself for me"*. Jesus loves me – heart, mind, body, soul, and every other part. I must love my wife the same way. When you love God much, you will also be freer to let your wife spend time with Him and with His work. I have had instances where I have needed my wife to be in bed with me either for just fellowship or for sexual intimacy, but she would be in another room for prayer. I learnt a long time ago not be jealous towards God or feel offended by this. I did not die for her. I did not save her soul. Jesus did. Let her express her love to Him and then come and express her love to me. If I love God, He is going to teach me how to love His daughter.

It is indeed a proven fact and truth that women generally gravitate towards love and words that express this. My spiritual father, the late Apostle Dr. E.H Guti says women have in their hearts this bottomless pit that must be filled with words, "I love you". This is rather hard for most men as we think our actions of working hard and providing for her are an expression of our love. To them it is not – it is our duty. There are things we can do to express our love for our wives – flowers, gifts, date nights, sexy lingerie, holidays, nice clothes and so forth. It is good and it must be done. But every day let her hear these three little words that may not mean much to some men but mean a whole world to our wives. So, learn to say it – "I LOVE YOU". Do not be like the other man who on New Year's Eve took a piece of white board and wrote with a marker – "I LOVE YOU x 365" and said to the wife – "See, don't ask me this coming year to say I LOVE YOU. I have already said it on this board for all the 365 days of this coming year". I very much suspect his New Years Eve did not go according to his plans!

I have always said to my friends that I want to love my wife so much that if I ever went to be with the Lord first, she is not ever going to remarry, for she will not find a man like me ever - in loving her and taking care of her.

#LoveHerTillSheMelts

CHAPTER 12

ADVICE TO WOMEN – SUBMIT AND DON'T TAKE HIM FOR GRANTED

> Ephesians 5 vs 22: *"Wives, submit to your own husbands, as to the Lord."*
> Colossians 3 vs 18: *"Wives, submit to your own husbands, as fitting in the Lord."*
> 1 Peter 3 vs 1: *"Wives, likewise, be submissive to your own husbands that even if some don't obey the word, they without a word, may be won by the conduct of their wives."*

Church doctrine is usually formed when two or more scriptures agree on the same thing. The issue of wives submitting to their husband is a command... full stop! Like in the previous chapter where men are being commanded to love their wives as Christ loved the church. Here wives are being commanded to submit to their own husbands. It is not a suggestion – it is a commandment. Wives are simply commanded to submit to their own husbands.

The first two scriptures above are from Apostle Paul writing to the church at Ephesus and at Colosse, but the third scripture is Apostle Peter writing to various Christians in Asia Minor. To show this is God's plan for marriage, the Holy Spirit inspired these two apostles to write the same thing. As we analyze the scripture, we note the following:

a) All three scriptures mention "own husband", not just any husband. So, a woman is not obligated to submit to any other husband except her own. (This is different from submitting to a spiritual leader on spiritual matters).

b) Two out of three scriptures mentioned "as to the Lord" or "as is fitting in the Lord". So, this means that a woman or wife is allowed to refuse to submit if what the husband is saying dishonors God or reviles her faith in Christ. In other words, if a husband asked his wife to do an ungodly thing, she has the spiritual right to say no. No man has the right to send his wife to Hell by asking or even forcing her to do anything that is contrary to the word of God. That is what "as to the Lord" or "as fitting to the Lord" means.

c) The third scripture from Apostle Peter states a truth that as a minister of the gospel, I have seen over and over again. This truth is that if a Christian wife is submissive and respectful to her husband, the husband is won over gradually. It is usually a waste of time when a wife prays for an unsaved husband whom she disdains, disrespects and dishonors. Obviously, the husband thinks if this is what Christianity is, I am better off without it.

YOUR MARRIAGE… HEAVEN OR HELL ON EARTH?

This issue of submission has long been resisted by many women, especially those of the woman's rights movement or the extreme feminists. But then Scripture is often not in step with popular opinion. The word of God remains supreme, and it depends on whether the lady in question wants to obey God and His Word or not. A wife cannot demand that her husband must love her without her submitting to him in as much as a husband cannot demand a wife to honor, respect and esteem him if he will not do his part of loving her as Christ loved the church. This is why both husband and wife must be bible believing people. The supreme Word of God is the common denominator. It is not about anyone's opinion or the world's ideas. So, both husband and wife must submit to the word of God. That is why Paul commands us not to be unequally yoked with unbelievers in 2 Corinthians 6 vs 14. What ladies must know is that there is power in submission and honor to their husbands. Men are wired in a way that they gravitate towards where they are honored and submitted to. For example, a man will normally feel attracted to and enjoy the company of his secretary at the office or his female subordinate who submits to him and respects him rather than the always screaming, shouting, arrogant, unsubmissive wife at home, no matter how much he loves her. He may love her, but he may feel she is impossible to live with because she does not give him what a man yearns for – honor through submission and respect.

No man wants to feel taken for granted. The same with women, but for a man it goes further because of this "little big thing" called "ego". Every man, saved or unsaved, has an ego. That is what makes him a man. It gives him a competitive edge. It makes him feel like a real man and drives him to perform in every area as a man. Ego wants the wife to say her husband is the best. Ego pushes a man to try and perform better in bed, work harder, and bring more money, buy his wife the latest car, dress her fashionably and supply her needs. Ego says to a man if Mr. Jones next door can buy his wife the latest BMW so can I. If his friend can take his wife for holidays - so can he. As men we sometimes say, "There is no man who puts on his trousers both legs at once; we all put on our trousers one leg at a time". In other words, I am not less of a man than any other.

Now if a woman submits and learns to rub her husband's ego the right way, she will reap great benefits. Because of ego, there is a tendency for a man to desire to be "the knight in shining armor" to the woman he loves. Submission and honor enhance this in a man. In African traditions of Southern Africa, each tribe and clan have a totem. This totem can be an animal or bird or part of the body like the heart. Each totem has a poem of praise or appreciation. One of the first things a newly married woman would do was to memorize this poem or chant of her new husband's totem. Every time the husband did good, she would thank him for this specific great deed and honor him, reciting his totem chant or praise. She would recite it loudly with ululation and maybe a small dance here and there. Now this would work on the psyche of the man positively. This is how the psychology worked out; the man as he hears his wife reciting his totem (and every African man is proud of his totem), he would feel great – like a king. But because of the way a man is wired he would think in his heart, "If this woman is so excited and is honoring me for bringing home an impala wait till I bring home sable." He would put all efforts into bringing home a big sable and his wife and children would enjoy meat for weeks. Because of the ululation and totem recital of the wife because of sable, he would determine in his heart to do even better and bring home at buffalo. So, it would go on and on and on.

I have noticed that the more my wife Gwen submits and honors me, loving her is so easy and I must do something to prove to her that her submission and honor towards me is not misdirected at all and it is not in vain, and as a man I find a way to show her that.

What is submission?

To understand biblical submission, we must first state what it is not. Submission is not that the wife is or should be used as a doormat. It does not mean the wife is inferior or less intelligent. In fact, many husbands have a wife with a higher IQ than them. But those wives must still submit. Submission does not mean a wife is less than the husband. No! We are equal before God. Our bodies, physical features, thinking patterns and emotions can be different, but we are equal. However, for order in the home, there must be a head – one head. We know that anything with two heads is a freak. One must lead in the home and God ordained man to lead – not by popular vote but by God's ordination – period!

Now that we accept that the man or husband must lead, the wife must follow – that is submission to the husband's leadership. Yes, she must help with well thought comments, suggestions, questions, contributions, remarks, and concerns when necessary, but she must never take the lead role. So, we ask again what is submission or to submit?

Submission is a humble attitude where obedience is rendered within a relationship, whether it is God, the boss at work, in church leadership or in this case in a marriage. The Greek word rendered "submit" in the bible gives the sense or means to "give way", to "yield". You choose to yield because it is the proper thing to do. Let's say you are driving the latest expensive super car like a Lamborghini, and you are on a side road about to enter a highway and a sign is written "Give Way" or "Yield" is facing you; from your right side on the highway an old model beaten up, cheap jalopy is rattling down the highway emitting smoke and all. Old, cheap, and smoky as it is, that old vehicle has right of way. That is the order. If you think to yourself and say, "how can I give way to an old rattling vehicle when I'm driving the newest and most expensive Lamborghini – let me take precedence and enter the junction first…" there is likely to be a big bang of an accident and your precious Lamborghini will be destroyed simply because you did not yield and give way; you did not submit to the rule of the road or the sign "Give Way or "Yield." You may even lose your life or write-off your expensive Lamborghini. This is the same in marriage. It is not about who is smarter. It is not about who earns more. It is not about who is more educated. It is about what the law of God (the Word) says. That is why unequal yoking in marriage is dangerous. You and your spouse will be operating by different rules in an unequal yoke so the non-believer between the two of you is not bound, neither do they see themselves obligated to operate according to the Word of God.

I want to reiterate the truth that submitting and honoring your husbands pays so many dividends. Let us look at 1 Peter 3 vs 5-6, it states, "For in this manner, in former times, the holy women who trusted God also adorned themselves, being submissive to their own husbands as Sarah obeyed Abraham calling him lord, whose daughters you are if you do good and are not afraid with terror."

Here Peter is telling or commanding wives that like godly women of old, they must also submit to their own husbands as Sarah obeyed and submitted to Abraham calling him lord. Note the word "lord" with lowercase "l" is from the Hebrew "adonai" with lower case "a". Now we need to remember the "Adonai" with capital "A" is a title for

God. It therefore means as God is "Adonai" to us all, Abraham was "adonai" to Sarah and hence a husband is "adonai" to his wife. In other words, Sarah honored Abraham and called him "lord" and her daughters, our wives are supposed to emulate her and treat us as "lord" or "adonai" as well. Right now, I can sense the tenseness in the women reading this but hear me out my sisters. As you can see scripture is clear on this. So, a wife must honor her husband as "adonai" with a small "a" or "lord" with a small "l".

What does "Adonai" mean apart from just Lord? Adonai means "Master" and "Owner" or "Lord, my Ruler." May I suggest that this is the case here in 1 Peter 3 vs 6 where Sarah calls Abraham "my lord" or "my ruler". In fact, scripture is full of verses where people honored others by calling them "adonai". For example, Aaron called Moses "adonai" (Numbers 12 v 11), Hazaal king of Syria called Elisha "adonai" (2 Kings 8 vs 12) and many more. Now, get me right, I am not necessarily advocating that wives call their husbands "lord", but I am advocating that just like in the scripture above, wives ought to honor their husbands. How is this profitable to the wife? Well, it is a double-edged sword.

Here is the balance and crux of the matter:
When we call God "Adonai" not only are we submitting to Him that He has leadership or rulership over us – but we are also saying that accordingly as "Master" and "Owner", all we have comes from him. He supplies everything to us. So, in the same vein, if a man is to be "adonai", he must act as one. What does God "Adonai" do for us? What did "adonai" Abraham do for Sarah? Whatever God does for the church, His bride and Abraham did for Sarah, so every husband must do for his wife for him to be a true "adonai". As husbands therefore, we cannot expect our wives to submit to us and honor us like Sarah

honored Abraham as lord without us acting and behaving accordingly to our wives. In other words, each "adonai" has duties to perform on his wife to make the lordship worthwhile and acceptable.

Here are the "adonai" duties of a husband:

1. Leadership – a husband must lead clearly, with love, patience, grace, and wisdom.
2. Provision – a master always provided ALL supplies for his servants. So, a husband must supply all his wife's needs whether she earns her own money or not. When money comes in, she must not lack her groceries, female needs, and grooming. Even the woman (mistress) of Proverbs 31 made sure that she supplied her servants with their portions (vs 15).
3. Faithfulness – a husband must be faithful and trustworthy. As God our Adonai is faithful, so must every husband be, as God's representative in the family. Every wife must be able to take her husband's word to the bank. We sing of God's faithfulness, so our wives must boast of our faithfulness as husbands as well. Marital faithfulness, financial faithfulness, and every other type of faithfulness.
4. Security – We know we are all secure in our great Adonai. In the same manner a husband must give his wife total security. Apart from love, women crave for security. There are many types of security that a woman needs:

    a) Spiritual security – Make sure the wife is really settled in God. Cover her with prayer.

Counsel her, teach her the word and encourage her on spiritual matters. Be a priest and pastor at home.

b) Financial security – fear of lack unsettles a woman. As "adonai", husband must strive to have multiple streams of income and provide finances.

c) Physical security – as God fights our battles, so must a husband physically protect his wife. Check the doors are locked before you go to sleep. Open the door if there is a knock and do not send her to answer the knock. Always check her seatbelt is on before you drive off or take off in a plane. If you are taking a walk in the neighborhood, and an angry dog comes to attack you, shield her with your body and deal with the dog. If she is on medication, remind her to take it. If she needs medical attention do not hesitate to drive her to the doctor after you pray for her.

d) Emotional security – Make sure she is emotionally stable. Keep her happy and laughing. She must have a sense of wellbeing. Help her to get out of bad moods and sadness. Never use the things she says when she is vulnerable in a fight (argument) or "intense moment of fellowship". When she opens her heart and says even things that may not make sense to you – do not laugh or judge. When she owns up to her weaknesses and mistakes do not emotionally hurt her by bringing it up again.

e) Material security – every wife deserves a nice house – a roof over her head, nice clothes on her back and wardrobe with nice clothes and food on the table. Budget for her wardrobe upgrade. Those shoes and handbags may be so many to you – but "adonai", be true to your title and buy for her. Supply her material needs. Build or buy a house she can call her own and graduate from renting. Let her eat what she wants when she wants… (hope she chooses healthy foods) … but lack must not be in the house.

As we close this chapter, I believe it is appropriate to say to us all – never take your spouse for granted. That spouse you take for granted; someone wishes that spouse was theirs. Taking each other for granted kills love.

#SubmitAndLetHimLead

CHAPTER 13

TEMPERAMENTS, PERSONALITIES AND CHARACTER

It is a well-known fact that a human being is three-in-one. A human being is a spirit, has a soul and lives in a body. The part that gets saved when we receive the Lord Jesus as our Lord and Savior is the spirit. With effort and dedication, we then need to work on the soul or 'psyche' in Greek, and discipline the body – the house we live in. We realize that a person can receive Jesus and love Him but if he/she does not work on their soul through prayer, reading the word and discipline he/she becomes a Christian with habits, emotions, and behaviors identical to those of any unsaved person. This is why Apostle Paul tells us in Philippians 2 vs 12 to work out our salvation with fear and trembling. The soul is the seat of the will, emotions, feelings and thought patterns. It is the home of temperaments, which together with other factors like background experiences, mold our personalities and character. Temperaments, personality, and character all contribute to how we behave or respond to people and situations around us. They certainly play a big role in relationships – including the marital relationship. Some disagreements and fights in a family are a result of personality, character flaws and/ or failure to understand each other's temperament.

What is a temperament?
A temperament is a person's nature which affects their behavior. There are temperaments that are in born. We also call them 'personality traits' and they determine how someone relates or reacts to the world. Your temperament plays a role in how you behave and interact with other people. Now, let no one say because they are inborn, temperaments cannot be changed. The word of God can change us. The Holy Spirit can change us. Do not say, "I was born this way", when your spouse is crying because of you. The Word of God says nothing is impossible with one who believes (Mark 9 vs 23). So, as long as we are willing, all of us can change.

Temperaments influence one's personality and that with other things, good or bad, that we learn in life (experience) – influence one's character. How we were raised plays a big role in character. Normally bad character is the default setting of people who were not disciplined in growing up. It is important to note that if the four temperaments are known, they have both positive and negative traits. Knowing what your temperament is allows the Holy Spirit to take away the negative aspects of it. It is not very possible for a spouse to change their partner if the partner does not want to change. However, if the partner desires to be a better person, the spouse can help by gently, graciously but very clearly pointing out what their partner needs to work on. Negative traits that cause grief must be gotten rid of.

YOUR MARRIAGE... HEAVEN OR HELL ON EARTH?

Here are the profiles of the four temperaments:

1. SANGUINE – "The Talker"
   Talkative, sociable, charismatic, outgoing, volatile, optimistic, cheerful, heart of every party, loves fun and action. Easily gets bored. Starts a project with passion, gets bored and wants to start something new with more fun. Loves attention. Impulsive, pleasure seeking. Carefree, expressive, desires influence, pleasant, lively, creative, compassionate, humorous. Attracts others quickly and makes friends quickly. Sincere at heart, always a child, colorful, great volunteer, thrives on compliments and does not hold grudges. Can be restless and spontaneous, loves luxury and travelling.

Because of being impulsive they find it hard to control their cravings and so are susceptible to smoking, alcohol, drugs and other addictions and mood disorder. Very poor in tolerating boredom. Avoid monotony at all costs. So cannot stand boring partners and takes them to be annoying and irritating. Extrovert and forward and bold, they seldom show signs of embarrassment. Always eager to be heard in a group, they love to express themselves. Good with details.

   ***Biblical examples** – King David and Apostle Peter.
   Color: Yellow

2. CHOLERIC – "The Driver" (Ambitious and leader-like)
   Type "A" personality – "The Doer" and "The Driver"- hard driving, hard to please, aggressive, energetic, and passionate and is surprised when others do not have the same passion and energy towards a goal as them. Dominant desire to

control and have authority. Determined, quick to act, fiery. This is the most insensitive of all temperaments...cares more for results (goals) instead of people. Strong willed, independent, self-sufficient, organizer, unemotional, thrives on opposition, is not easily discouraged! Does not do well in a subordinate position. Skeptical and does not trust easily. Needs to investigate facts on their own, bossy, and domineering. Cannot relax, impatient, quick tempered, easily angered, cruel sometimes and unsympathetic. Enjoys arguments, dominates people of other temperaments. Workaholic and in charge of everything. Want their way or no way. Highly independent with high standards. Perseveres always.

- desire facts not emotions.
- does not have many friends.
- tendency to fall into deep sudden depression and mood swings
- forward and bold.
- insists on their ideas being accepted.
- not emotionally expressive except through anger.
- conceited, can deceive or disguise.

*Many people of this temperament are military generals and politicians.

Biblical examples: Apostle Paul, James, Titus, and Martha. Color: Red

3. MELANCHOLIC – "The Thinker."

Serious, anxious, quiet, fearful, depressed, poetic, artistic, sad, introverted, and thoughtful. Called "The Thinker" because they are analytical, cautious and restrained. Pessimistic deep thinkers, who often tend to see the negative attributes of life, rather than the positive. Self-reliant and independent, they get completely involved in what they are doing. Can be highly creative in art, literature, music, health care and ministry. They tend to dwell on the tragedy and cruelty in the world and desire to solve those issues. Genius prone and perfectionists. Have deep love for others but usually having contempt for themselves. Experience deep bouts of depression that come from dissatisfaction and disappointments. They are serious, sometimes too serious with life. Because they deeply care, they make great doctors, nurses, social workers, ministers, and teachers. Loyal friend – but have low self-image and always feeling guilty due to timidity. Bashful and easily embarrassed and refrain from talking in a group. They are good with details, deliberate, over-cautious, reserved, compliant and yielding, distant, crosses bridges before coming to them. Secretive, seclusive, modest and often represent themselves at a disadvantage. They are frequently moody and gloomy and easily hurt.

***Biblical Examples:** Abraham, Moses, and Elijah.
Color: Blue

4. PHLEGMATIC – "The Watcher".
Slow, introvert, patient, calm, quiet, shy, rational, and consistent. Relaxed, warmly attentive and lazily sluggish. Observant – they are referred to as "The Watcher." Steady, good at mediation and unity. They are mostly female – content with self, easy-going, cool, and collected. They are tolerant to others, well balanced,

sympathetic, kind, keep emotions hidden, never in a hurry, avoids conflict, inoffensive, quiet but witty and agreeable and so has many friends. Though peaceful, they tend to be reluctant, indecisive and tend to worry. Good at generalizing things – seeing the bigger picture and reading between the lines and prefer stability to change. Compromising nature due to fearfulness and indecision. They desire to know the innermost part of a person and know themselves better. They persevere and display a constant mood. Slow in movement. On the negative side, phlegmatics are often selfish, self-righteous, judge others, easily resist change, aloof and dampen others enthusiasm. They are also passive-aggressive.

***Biblical Examples:** Joseph, Timothy, and Barnabas.
Color: Green

Now without making this chapter unnecessarily long, let us ponder on the four temperaments here. It is obvious that many problems in marriage can be brought about by the spouses' temperaments. For example, the phlegmatics can cause the spouse to feel unfairly treated, always delayed and unsupported... and the dampening of the spouse enthusiasm!

The melancholic's moody disposition can end up being irritating and troublesome to the spouse. What about the pessimism and negativity? Then the self-blame and guilt-trips? It is hard to be in such company!

Let us bring in the cruel tendencies of the choleric, the lack of care when he/she hurts others due to concern and focus on achievements without care for people. We can mention the domineering, argumentativeness and insensitivity of this temperament. Who would love to be in such company?

Then my team, my buddies – the Sanguines ...always talking, always pursuing fun, always on the go, always wanting attention and are volatile. This is the group that wants everyone to also hear what they are thinking whether invited to do so or not. They tend to love the sound of their own voices! What can we do with these?

The above are just a few factors of each temperament. Unless one is willing to change and shed the negative side of their temperament, the marriage is always at risk of being in problems. Jesus came to redeem and deliver us completely so that we can have life in abundance and in its fulness (Greek: 'zoe'). Each husband and each wife must desire to let go of the negative aspects of their temperament and only keep the positive aspects. God can help us through the Holy Spirit who burns the chaff away. Identify your character and personality flaws caused by either your background or your temperament and get rid of them. God the Father, Jesus the Son and the Holy Spirit are willing to help us change, and they are very capable. Are you willing to change? Are you willing to let go of the negative attributes you have that your spouse has been complaining about, warning, and telling you that you have such?

We need grace. Can you imagine two Cholerics getting married and failing to change? What about a Phlegmatic and a Melancholic? It would be a house of sadness and boredom. Two Sanguines together...exhausting!

I think you get the point! Let us work on our temperaments, personalities, and character. Nothing is impossible. Again, let us heed

Apostle Paul in Philippians 2:12 who says, "Therefore my beloved, as you have always obeyed, not as in my presence only, but now much more in my absence, work out your own salvation with fear and trembling." I rest my case!

#DesireToChange

CHAPTER

14

BIRDS OF A FEATHER... CHOOSING FRIENDS AS A COUPLE

In 2 Corinthians 6 v 4 Apostle Paul writes, "*Do not be unequally yoked with unbelievers...*" Some are married but do not really believe in marriage or its sanctity. Some like the feeling of being married but are not prepared to do the hard work. In other words, we can say they are not really believers in the institution of marriage. Stay away from such unbelievers. Many even call themselves Christians but because of some hurts in the past they have a negative view of marriage – yet they are married. It is also unwise for a married woman to have friends who are single as close confidantes. The same with the husband. Choose friends who value marriage like you or more than you. It is said, "show me your friends and I will show you your future". Birds of a feather flock together. Like-minded people stick together. Couples of like-minds stick together. If you stick around the wrong crowd, it will not be long before their lousy attitude catches up with you whether you like it or not. When you hear their negative talk about their spouses or marriage in general it will stick with you whether you like it or not.

A wife who wants to experience all that God has for her marriage runs away from women who trash talk their husbands, their in-laws or marriage in general. They love the sex in marriage but do not like the work they have to put into the relationship. As a wife, if you have a friend who always talks bad about her husband or his family – run away from that "friend", she is not a genuine friend, my sister. Marriage can be tough. You need encouragers and those who inspire you – not the opposite. Choose your friends well. Also check whether your husband's friends hold marriage in high esteem. I say again, do not be in the company of women who disrespect their husbands and in-laws. They are toxic to your marriage. Married or single friends who consider marriage as a necessary evil are not your portion.

Similarly, as a husband if you happen to have a friend who dishonors his wife or disrespects her, run for your dear life. A friend who dishonors his wife privately or publicly is not a true friend. A friend who makes fun of his wife is not worthy of your friendship or your time. A friend who discusses his wife's weaknesses when you are not that couple's counselor is not a valid friend. A friend who shows the attitude that for him being single is better than being married will probably divorce soon to realize "his dream". A man who confides in people that he married the wrong woman is in turn the wrong friend to have. A guy who talks trash about his in laws is no friend of yours. They may be bad in-laws but hanging his family's dirty linen in public is both a sign of ignorance and it is evil.

So, what shall we say? A wise couple must choose friends that benefit their marriage. A sensible couple should not deal with couples or individuals who give them extra baggage by what they say of each other or each other's in-laws. It is also important to have friends who love fun and are outgoing. They help keep your marriage fresh. Have friends who are always young at heart. Friends must inspire friends. Friends must encourage friends, therefore, have friends who invite, persuade or even force you to invest in your spouse and in your marriage. Good friends direct you to godly principles in marriages. They encourage you to tithe, to give, to serve God, to minister in the house of God with your substance and your time. Great friends encourage each other's walk with God. They challenge each other to do good work in church and in the community and to the in-laws. Great friends will drag you to a marriage seminar or retreat even when somehow you have decided not to attend. That's what great friends do. That's what good friends strive to do all the time.

Now, as a couple or as a husband or wife, please take careful stock of your friends and acquaintances. Those who do not inspire and encourage you, say bye-bye to them. Help your spouse gently and with well-chosen words to point out his/her friends you feel are toxic to him/her or to your relationship as a whole. Choose your friends well.

#FriendsMatter

CHAPTER

15

FRUITFULNESS AS A COUPLE

On our wedding day, my pastor and marriage celebrant preached from John 12 vs 24. It says, *"Most assuredly I say to you, unless a grain of wheat falls into the ground and dies, it remains alone. But if it dies, it produces much grain."* My then pastor was teaching Gwen and I that the 'me, myself, and I' in us must die and then we could bear fruit as a couple – one couple – two becoming one. The teaching is that unless each of us died to self, we would not be fruitful.

This truth is relevant to EVERY spouse in marriage, but it is also vital for a couple in a church or in the community. We grow by dying to self and seeing the needs around us, the needs in the church we attend and the needs in our community. A couple – more so a Christian couple, must be fruitful. We must bear fruit. I am not talking about children here (biological children) – I am talking about a life of productivity in this world. A good or blessed couple must minister in their church one way or the other. Surrender your home to be a meeting place for home bible study group or prayer meeting. Volunteer to host visiting speakers at your church without expecting the church to give you money for the guests' food. Teach children's church. Employ your talents in the praise and worship team. Volunteer to clean the church sanctuary or pay for a professional cleaner to do that. Minister to your pastor and teach your children the same. Be the go-to-couple for other couples needing counseling, financial help, and sympathy for the bereaved. Be a blessing when a brother or sister weds in your church. Help where and when necessary.

When in Genesis 1 vs 28 *God said to Adam and Eve, "Be fruitful and multiply..."* He just was not only talking about biological reproduction... that was only a small part of it. God repeats that same command to Noah in Genesis 9 vs 7 and says, "And as for you be fruitful and multiply. Bring forth abundantly in the earth and multiply in it". If we think that a couple's major purpose is to have children, then we are the most miserable of all creations. We need to understand this goes far beyond the biological multiplication. God is a God of multiplication. He multiplies a seed into a forest or a field of corn or wheat. By repeatedly sowing, the seed dying and germinating and bearing much fruit again, multiplication continues. That fruit is sown, and the cycle repeats itself into a super-abundance.

A couple must sow always. Sow your time and energy into evangelism or some other ministry. Sow money and prosper. Sow love and receive love. Sow, sow, sow! Multiply, multiply, multiply. Through Adam and Eve, every couple was given the mandate to multiply. God multiplies. In John 10 vs 34, Lord Jesus quotes the psalmist David in Psalm 82 vs 6 where it is written, "I said you are gods, and all of you are children of the Most High!" So, you and I are gods (note – lower-case 'g'.) And we are sons of the Most High. Like

Father, like son. Even as a female you are a "son", in the spirit. The Bible talks about "sons of God". The gender 'her' is irrelevant. The point here is, God multiplies, He commanded us to multiply and so we must multiply.

Our spiritual gifts and our anointing must multiply as a couple. Our ministerial abilities must multiply. Our personal finances must multiply. Our substance must multiply so that we use them for the Kingdom of God. Our influence must multiply. We must pray the prayer of Jabez of asking God to enlarge our tents (1 Chronicles 4 vs 9-10). God expects us to – and he tells us again in Isaiah 54 vs 32 – *"Enlarge the place of your tent and let them stretch out the curtains of your dwellings..."* Verse 3 then starts with *"For you shall expand to the right and to the left."* It is clear – God wants us to grow, to expand, to multiply.

As a couple, we must always check and see whether we are growing and multiplying. People are attracted to us and to the God we serve when they see us multiply and not be stagnant. I am not saying that for Christian couples everything will always flow...no, that is not what I mean. There are always times of tests and trials. Even in marriage. But the promises of God are yes and amen in Christ Jesus. A couple must see progress in their lives so others can eat the fruit that they bear. I like what Paul says to Timothy in 1 Timothy 4vs 15, "Meditate on these things, give yourself entirely to them, that your progress may be evident to all." Our progress must be evident to all.

As a couple, spur each other on into multiplication! As couples with good friends, spur each other on to multiplication.

#Multiply

CHAPTER

16

INFLUENCING AND HELPING OTHERS

In Genesis 12, God told Abraham that the nations of the world would be blessed through him. Part of the Abrahamic blessing which we as Christians enjoy is being blessed to bless others. Your marriage as a couple must inspire others. As a Christian couple your marriage must influence other couples and impact them in a positive way.

Jabez, in 1 Chronicles 4 vs 9-10, prays the prayer that God blesses him and enlarges his tents or territory. He was asking God to enlarge his influence. As Christian couples we must pray such types of prayers. We must be influencers. We must ask God to use us to bring the joy of great marriages into people's lives. To make this happen, we must not only just talk the talk, but walk the walk. People who do not know God must see the goodness of God and His grace upon our lives. As they get close to us, we must make deliberate efforts to draw them close and be able to give input into their lives and marriages. God blesses us to be a blessing. When we see struggling couples, we should be able to counsel them and help them and be a good example to them. We cannot give what we do not have. But when God has given us grace in our marriage, we surely must minister to others even if we are still growing and maturing ourselves. We do not have to wait until our marriages are perfect – if there is anything called a perfect marriage. In giving time and counsel to others in need, God increases us, so we can minister at a much higher and more effective level. Scriptures that back this up are: "He who waters will himself be watered" in Proverbs 11 vs 25; and "Give and it shall be given back to you," from Luke 6 vs 38.

Evangelists come in different ways. Each one of us is called to win souls. If God can use my marriage to win souls, what an honor and a blessing that would be! So, help other couples. Be a hostess. Let them know that once upon a time you also struggled in a certain area and God gave you grace to overcome. Get real. Do not make other couples feel that you had it made from the start. Gwen and I are effective in couple ministry because though we are enjoying a very blessed marriage, we do not hesitate to self-reveal or self-disclose. This is when we openly talk of our previous mistakes, disagreements and struggles and how we overcame them. This makes other couples realize that there is indeed hope. Let us not give people the impression that all has been perfect.

We must not allow couples to give up on their marriages. We must help them fight for what God has for them – the very best! We must be careful though. In fighting for other people's marriages, we must not entangle ourselves as a couple that it impacts on us negatively. We must be wary of what is called 'vicarious burnout'. Vicarious burn out is experienced by counselors and other helpers when they become so personally involved in their counseling issues that they

are weighed down by those issues. This can render them exhausted or can lead to depression. In the case of couples, stress from helping others can cause fights between the helping couple.
In psychology, there is what is called "transference" and 'countertransference' Transference is when the counselee, the struggling couple in this case, somehow manage to "mirror" their problems on the counseling (helping) couple. It is up to the helping couple to avoid this. It can be subtle, but you sense the struggling couple sort of projecting their issues on you. Countertransference is when the helping couple may be going through an issue themselves and allow the "vibes" or negative issues to affect the counselees.

It is true that it is not always easy, but remember the more you help others, the more God equips you and blesses your marriage.

#BlessedToBeABlessing

CHAPTER

17

DEALING WITH CHILDREN

"Children are a heritage from the Lord, the fruit of the womb is a reward" Psalm 127 vs 3.

This scripture clearly shows us that it is God who blesses us with children. Many a time we take this for granted and expect that every couple, when they marry and desire children - will have them. It is not so. Some couples struggle to eventually have children. Others never have them. Some have them but are disappointed with the timing. Others even call some of their children "accidents" – which is wrong. God is the One who gives children. Gwen and I are one couple who had to wait and pray for the blessing of the fruit of the womb – for 3 years! When my spiritual father and mentor, the late Apostle Dr Ezekiel H. Guti prayed for Gwen and I to conceive in early February 1992, God did a miracle and blessed us with a baby boy in October of that year. Others have waited longer than us and many are still waiting. This means we must not take the blessing of children for granted.

However, we must also realize that lack of children in a marriage does not render that marriage less important or inferior by any manner. It is therefore important for the couple still waiting for this blessing to realize that as a couple you are a family, and children are additions – precious welcomed additions but nonetheless additions. A couple must enjoy life and enjoy each other, while they are awaiting the blessing of children. At no point and in no circumstance must they feel inadequate because they have no children – even though that is exactly what the devil tries, with many tactics, to make them feel. I vividly remember times when Gwen's period would somehow be delayed and that raised our hope that she had conceived, only for her to realize it was just a delayed period and she had not conceived. She would be filled with disappointment, anguish, and a sense of inadequacy. She told me she did not feel "woman enough." That was the lie of the devil.

For those who are blessed with children, no matter how long it took to receive the blessing, we have the godly obligation to raise these children in the fear of God. Children are a great responsibility but a welcome one to most. It is vital for a couple to make sure the spiritual needs of their children are well catered for. It starts while they are still in the womb. Both parents, but more so the father, must pray for the child as soon as it is conceived. I remember laying hands on Gwen's womb and blessing my son and interceding for him before he was born. He would always respond by moving in the womb.

Psalms 58 vs 3 says, *"The wicked are estranged in the womb. They go astray as soon as they are born, speaking lies."* The RSV says, *"The wicked go astray from the womb, they err from birth speaking lies."* I do not know how you personally interpret this scripture but the way I see it is that the devil attacks children from the womb and they come out already with a propensity to do evil. We see the issue of Jacob who comes out of the womb holding his elder brother's heel, thus earning him his name Jacob, meaning "thief" or "Supplanter." Sure enough, he stole his brother's birthright. I know some will argue that this was God's plan as prophesied earlier, but the point is that Jacob came out a thief, a dubious character. So, it is important to pray for our pregnant wives and the babies in the womb as soon as conception is confirmed. I believe that the opposite to this scripture is true as well – that is, "the righteous go righteous in the womb, they come out prophesying and declaring the salvation of God". I believe that the laying on of hands by the father and the targeted prayers of the mother on the unborn baby will reverse Psalms 58 vs 3 to a positive outcome.

It is the obligation and responsibility of the parents as a couple to expose their offspring to the gospel of Jesus Christ at a very early age. It is a must for couples to lay hands and bless their children often and speak salvation and success over them. Allow your pastor to lay hands on your children like Jesus did in Matthew 19. Create a godly atmosphere in the home for the child to learn godliness. Discipline is paramount, even corporal, no matter what the world and politicians say. There are over five verses in Proverbs that talk of disciplining children. Do not be fooled by the world. Do it reasonably and lovingly. Do not wait until it is too late and let the police, the prosecutor, the judge, and the prison system do the discipline for you. That would be too late already. Psychologists agree that a child learns all they will ever need to use in life from zero to age seven. If you do not sow the right seed in your child at this age you are courting disaster for your offspring.

Train your child in godly ways. Teach them, drill into them to love God with all their faculties. "Train up a child in the way that they should go and when they are old they won't depart from it" (Proverbs 22 v 6). Do not leave all the responsibility to the children's teacher at your church. Remember the Sunday School teacher has at most two hours on a Sunday with your child, but you have hours on end, seven days a week with them. Ask your children what is going on at kindergarten or school. Ask them what they learnt at Sunday School. Be involved. Don't ever be too busy for your children. You will regret it. Do not allow TV to raise your children and regulate sleep overs... Never expose your child to what you are not sure of. What music does your child have at home? Do you do bible study? Do you pray with them? It is not good for a child to hear her father 'speaking in tongues' only at church. Let them hear you pray in tongues at home too and pray for them. Lay hands on them before they go to bed. Give them memory verses to say each morning before they go to school. Never talk negatively or backstab the brethren at church or your pastor while your children are listening. It is bad enough for you to speak negatively about fellow believers but doing it with them or in their presence or within the earshot of your child is a disservice to your own child. You put a bad seed in them. They will take you as a hypocrite – taking them to church to meet the pastor and the people you do not like or love. They will also reason for themselves and conclude that it is not worth going to church because there are bad people there. Do not sabotage your own family by talking nonsense about church, or anything connected with God. Do not kill your children spiritually.

Teach your children the correct godly core values including tithing. Let them know that *"What shall it profit a man if he should gain the whole world but lose his soul?"* (Matthew 16 vs 26). *Do it "precept upon precept, line upon line, here a little there a little,"* according to Isaiah 28 vs 10. Never leave anything to chance. The devil is fighting to win your children over. We therefore need plenty of God's grace, but it needs our efforts too. There is a time when you will have to drag your teenage children to church but if in the early years the foundation was strong you do not need to fear. Proverbs 15 vs 22 will always stand true. God's word does not lie.

Communication between parents and children is important. Learn new things. Also allow the children to educate you on what they feel and what they are going through - peer pressure, bullying, the fight to be popular on social media and so on. Communicate, communicate, communicate! Hear them out. As parents let us not be dictators. Admit when wrong. Learn to apologize to your children when necessary, I have done that to my children several times. Let us not allow pride to dominate us as parents. There must be times when we are vulnerable. Let our children know that we are human too and apologizing is a way of teaching them humility, honesty, and integrity. Be united when disciplining children. If they sense division between the two of you, they take advantage of that, and the battle is lost before you begin. Neither father nor mother should try to win the children's "good graces" at the expense of the other partner or the child himself. If you disagree on an issue of discipline at hand do the talking and disagreeing privately but always present a united front before the children. Also be alert to the type of toys you buy your children. Desist from violent toys, or toys that bring demons into the child. Is every toy necessary? Some parents try to overcompensate for their failure to spend time with their children by loading them with toys and expensive clothes. What will that profit them? Everything must be done in moderation.

Now when it comes to the physical raising of children, the man must be as involved as the wife. The time is long gone when child rearing was left to the wife alone. Most women work and contribute to the household income. It is only fair for the husband to be hands-on too in childcare. I am glad that God gave me grace in this area. I am proud to mention that I was physically present when all my three children were born. I bathed all three, bottle fed and even spoon fed all three! I babysat all three. I have always been, and I still am involved in their lives. When my second born Bethany wedded, I helped run around with errands for the wedding – even the female stuff like gown etc. I did not just start now, it started when they were born. Now Bethany and her husband have a baby boy. I was at the maternity ward when my grandson was born. Not only that, but I also took a "shift" in taking care of my precious grandson at night. Children will always appreciate when we help them even in their adulthood.

It is not fair when husbands complain that their wives make them late for church or appointments when the poor lady must bathe and dress and feed the toddler when the father is reading a newspaper online or flipping through TV channels. A good husband, a husband of today, takes care of his children in every way possible – even cooking for them. As a man, do you do homework with your children? Do you even show interest in their schoolwork? Are you concerned about their mental well-being? Do you reassure them of your love? Do you reassure them when they have self-doubt? Are your children free to tell you what is going on in their school or in their lives generally? It is only when you make yourself available as a father that they can unburden their secrets on you so that you can help and guide them the right way. Children are a precious blessing, but they also come with great responsibilities physically, emotionally, and spiritually. Let me ask you a question my fellow husband, are you involved in the life and affairs of all your children?

#ChildrenAreABlessing
#TheModernFatherCares

CHAPTER

18

BODILY EXERCISE PROFITS

In 1 Timothy 4 vs 8 (KJV), Apostle Paul states that *"bodily exercise profiteth a little"*. On reading the rest of the verse, you realize that Paul was not saying that bodily exercise is worthless; he was simply comparing bodily exercise and spiritual things in this case, godliness which he said is "profitable unto all things". We can therefore conclude that godliness and other spiritual disciplines that enhance our relationship with God must come first but it does not mean we have to ignore the physical body.

We must always remember that the body is the temple of the Holy Spirit (1 Corinthians 6:19). Therefore, it must be kept healthy and in good shape. When we wreck our bodies, the spirit within us cannot stay and departs (death). As Dr. Myles Munroe used to say, "It is illegal for a spirit to be on earth without a body". That is why even demons live in people and animals, like in Mark 5, where they begged Jesus that they be sent into the swines that were nearby. A couple must endeavor to have a healthy and long life. God gives us life and knows when we will depart this earth, but a lot of people are departing from earth before time because they did not take care of their bodies. Eating well, avoiding fatty foods and so on is vital. Resting, getting enough sleep, and exercising keeps the body strong and healthy and produces longevity.

It is also interesting to note that couples that exercise regularly and have fit bodies enjoy sex more than those that do not exercise. Sex itself demands stamina and the stronger the body, the more enjoyable sex is. Strong bodies can have several rounds of explosive sex without tiring. If a couple wants to have the best sex ever, they ought to exercise and be fit. We have heard of couples who experience muscle cramps while having sex because they were out of shape. Others fail to have sex in certain positions because they experience discomfort and pain from lack of exercise. A few older men have had heart attacks during sex, especially when their spouses were much younger and sexually intense. Big, fat tummies are an impediment to good sex. For men, lack of exercise and eating junk food can also cause erectile dysfunction. Fat deposits line up the inside of the blood vessels of the penis and restrict the flow of blood to the penis. Since it is the abundance of blood in the penis blood vessels that causes an erection, failure of enough blood to reach "downstairs" cause the penis to fail to 'get to attention'. A doctor once told me that erectile dysfunction caused by fat in the body is a sign that soon this man will have heart problems because, if the fat gathers in the penis blood vessels it also gathers in all other vessels making the circumference of arteries smaller (narrow) and the heart has to work much harder to "force" blood through those restricted blood vessels. This eventually takes a toll on the heart resulting in all sorts of heart problems.

Sluggish sex is no fun! I am a firm believer that sex must be thoroughly enjoyed as a gift given to us in marriage by God. For many, exercise also brings a sense of wellbeing and with that a higher libido – and the bedroom performance becomes awesome too! Therefore, couples ought to influence each other to exercise. Take brisk walks, jog, ride bikes or go to the gym – doing something for physical exercise is vital!

#FitEnoughToRockAllNight

CHAPTER

19

KEEP BOUNDARIES

"When He gave the sea its boundary so the water would not overstep His command...." Proverbs 8 vs 29 (NIV).

Boundaries in life are vital – even in marriage. God is a God of boundaries. He s et boundaries so that there is order. The scripture above shows how God set the boundaries of the sea. When a tsunami hits and the sea goes beyond its boundaries, there is always chaos and destruction. Some things in nature and life in general are best kept in their prescribed domain, with very clear boundaries.

In marriage, a couple is supposed to set and maintain boundaries – whether at church or in the community. There must be boundaries to the type of jokes to entertain. There must be boundaries to familiarity with church members and members of the community. A couple must be dignified and not be loose. We must always be good representatives of the church and its godly doctrines. A man married or unmarried must be very vigilant of the extent he goes to in talking or fellowshipping with women. The same with women towards all men. Flirting has led either party in marriage to stray away and commit adultery. A couple without boundaries are easily seduced by the enemy. A couple must enjoy life and have fun, but it is vital to choose what type of fun to have. If it is sinful then it is not fun...it is death. How do you relate to people as a couple or individual? What do you do in your spare time when no one is watching? What books do you read? What movies do you watch?

There must be boundaries in the manner a couple earns money. It must not be by "hook-or-crook". There must be a boundary on what you use your money for. Do you expect God to bless you with more money when you use it for dodgy things? When you live with relatives in your home, have boundaries on how you interact with them. In the Shona culture of Zimbabwe, brothers-in-law and sisters-in-law customarily jest with each other and jokingly call each other husband or wife. Unfortunately, this jesting for many has led to flirting, and the flirting has led to sexual relations. We have heard of men who slept with their wife's sister. We have also heard of wives who slept with their husband's brother. This is not exclusive to Shona culture. Even Herod Antipas took his brother Phillp's wife (Herodias) in the bible and John the Baptist rebuked him leading to John's arrest and his subsequent execution.

Maintain boundaries at your workplace. Not every work colleague has a pure agenda towards you. Gwen and I once counseled a couple where the husband had become too close to a female work colleague and the vigilant wife noticed it and came to us to help her convince her husband to drop this female "friend". The husband had failed to set boundaries and was oblivious of the woman's motive and intention. The husband did not completely accept our counsel, thinking that his wife was simply jealous of his friendship. The truth came out at an office Christmas party when he went to this party with his wife. When the other woman, the so-called friend, saw him with his wife, she went berserk. She swore and cursed – saying how stupid he was to come to the Christmas party with his wife because she had planned that after the party, one way or the other she was going to have sex with him – come hail or thunder! So, he was saved by going to the party with his wife. Only then did he realize he had misread this woman's motive and that his wife was right all along.

Do you discuss your bedroom activities with your friends? If so, you lack boundaries. People at work must know you for what you stand for and for what you will not compromise with. Life may be full of pitfalls; we must not add more by failing to have boundaries.

#SafetyInBoundaries

CHAPTER

20

THE UGLY TRUTHS ABOUT DIVORCE

Malachi 2 vs 16 states, *"For the LORD of Israel says that He hates divorce for it covers one's garment with violence"*.

Divorce in most cases is nasty. It is evil, especially where children are involved. But children or no children, divorce is painful. God hates divorce. Jesus said that there is no reason for divorce except adultery. That is, if one of the spouses commits adultery thereby breaking the marriage vow, the grieved spouse can divorce him/her but better still you can forgive and move ahead if possible. But what if the offender repeats infidelity? At such a point you cannot blame a spouse for divorce if his /her spouse does not repent, change and work to win back trust and be of integrity. You cannot ask a spouse to continue with a serial adulterer or adulteress.

YOUR MARRIAGE... HEAVEN OR HELL ON EARTH?

In the bible, I have never seen an incident where a man is said to have physically or verbally abused his wife or vice versa. Thus, according to the Bible, I believe, this makes adultery the only reason for divorce. But this world has become worse and worse. Husbands beat up their wives and vice versa. Some husbands are even murdering their spouses. This then makes it obviously sensible that the abused partner can and should file for divorce. It would not be fair to sentence someone's daughter or son to a lifetime of physical abuse, even psychological abuse such as 'gas lighting' and verbal abuse that demeans someone and diminishes them as a person. Some spouses have gone through mental torture, others even financial abuse. It would be callous to insist that under such circumstances (when the offending spouse does not change) that a spouse must remain under these conditions.

Truth be told, divorce still hurts. One divorced man once said that divorce is like one of your arms has been cut off. Most divorces are so acrimonious, involving parents and relatives of the divorcing couple, and breaking the hearts of the children, often tearing these children apart as their loyalties may differ. Even friends of the divorcing couple get affected as some couples (friends) end up arguing in their homes on which spouse in the divorcing couple was right and who was wrong and who caused the divorce. Loyalties can do damage as the divorcing wife may be telling her female friends one story and the divorcing husband is telling his male friends a completely different story. Most of the time, none of the two is willing to admit their mistakes. Couples (friends) get confused. Some will support the wife, and others will support the husband and some friends end up feeling that their spouse has betrayed them by supporting the other spouse and not the spouse they sympathize with. In a group of couples who were friends with the divorcing couple, some may even stop talking to each other because one couple thinks that their friends are supporting the wrong person in this marital dispute. What a fall out! That said and done, it is important to know that no couple in their right mind goes into marriage with the intention of someday getting divorced. That would not be normal or sane by any measure. And yet, many couples end up in the divorce court. Why?

The major reasons for divorce apart from infidelity and abuse are unfulfilled dreams and expectations, lack of sex, disagreements about money, and bad communication. Lack of wisdom also plays a big part in all this. Proverb 24 vs 3-4 advises that, "By wisdom a house is built and by 'understanding' it is established; by knowledge the rooms are filled with all precious and pleasant riches". Many marriages break down due to lack of wisdom of one or both spouses. This is why every couple must operate their marriage according to the Word of God and must pray. The devil celebrates when couples divorce especially Christian couples. We must confound the devil by making our marriages the best they can be. Let us endeavor to make our marriages fool-proof.

In other words, both husband and wife must determine that they are into this for keeps and work hard to get their marriage strong. Later in life, when good communication, great sex, wise handling of money and in-laws have been mastered, and the default habit of a couple are marriage investments through counseling, seminars, teachings, reading and deliberate service to one another have now become an integral part of their life, that marriage will never die. Say no to divorce and say yes to a life-long time in the holy matrimony. Move 'toward marital bliss'...as my wife Gwen entitled her 21-day marriage devotional book for women.

YOUR MARRIAGE… HEAVEN OR HELL ON EARTH?

#UntilDeathDoUsPart

CHAPTER 21

THE IMPORTANCE OF A COUNSELOR

Many couples and individuals in general think that counseling is only for those in a bind, a fix, a crisis. As a result, people, couples included, suffer unnecessarily because, for them going for counseling means that they are in a crisis, and they do not want people to think that they are in a crisis. This is very unprogressive and unprofitable thinking. In the multitude of counsellors there is safety. Without counseling, plans go awry as scriptures say.

Often this resistance to counseling is caused by ignorance or pride or both. More often than not, wives are more open to counseling, but their husbands may refuse because as they say, they "don't want their business out there". This is dangerous thinking. How can you sink with the ship because of pride? As long as you can find a discrete, ethical counselor, whatever you say in the counseling session stays in the counseling room. I have been a trained Christian counselor for over thirty years, and I also hold a Master's degree in professional counseling. The basic ethics training is the same to the most counselors, and that is – "what happens in Vegas stays in Vegas". Similarly, what happens in the counseling office stays in the counseling office. In fact, for a counselor to reveal what happens in counseling is not only unethical but is professionally wrong and criminally liable. A professional counselor can be prosecuted for revealing what happened in the counseling room.

So, every couple must look for a good Christian counselor even before things go awry. Gwen and I have, for years, done premarital counseling to prepare young couples for marriage before they wed. It has yielded phenomenal results. As mentioned before, we strongly believe that it is wrong when couples spend months planning for a wedding which only lasts a few hours instead of planning for the marriage which must last for a lifetime. Generally, in this area, priorities have been set wrong. It is better to invest in the marriage through premarital counseling than to only invest in the wedding itself. Many nicely planned glamorous weddings have been celebrated, but the couple may still end up separating or divorcing. This is because it is not about how well planned or glamorous the wedding was, it is about how prepared the couple are to living together and doing life together.

So, from the onset, a couple must seek counseling. Even if there is nothing wrong within a marriage, the discovery through counseling that you are doing it right can be a very encouraging and satisfying feeling for a couple. It is better to have preventative counseling than crisis counseling. Why allow the pain and the damage when you can avoid it? In fact, in many circumstances a couple that goes for regular counseling when there is no crisis, avoid crisis. Counseling is good for couples and good for individuals, so do not ever underestimate its power for couples. We have also come to realize that there are instances where a husband is open to counseling and the woman is not. I have encountered such couples in the counseling room. It is not only stupid but unreasonable for a wife to refuse counseling because, if that marriage ends up in divorce usually it is the wife who suffers more than the husband. And most husbands can quickly remarry while a divorced wife normally ends up stigmatized. Life is unfair that way but there is not much we can do about it.

When in crises do not hesitate to go for marital counseling, but I say – go for it before you get into a crisis. Avoid pain, argument, and sleepless nights when God has provided counselors in this world for you. Let every couple know that going for counseling is not a sign of weakness but wisdom. Do not wait until it is too late as some couples do. Some couples go for counseling when it is too late to salvage anything. It is important at this juncture to reveal that some counseling is actually training to handle situations in life. So, when you are well trained you can handle challenges that come your way because you were trained in counseling.

In counseling we teach couples to learn to de-escalate arguments instead of escalating them and we teach how to handle your communication, sex, money, in-laws, and everything else. The famous marriage psychologist Dr. John Gottman has separated couples into two general groups – the "masters of marriage" and the "disasters of marriage". There are things that the "masters" of marriage do that make their marriages flourish and things that they avoid. "disasters" handle their relationship badly. However, with counseling and a couple willing to learn and unlearn other habits, the "disasters" can become "masters" too. All this happens through counseling. It is important for us all to remember that no one was "born married". We all live single lives then marry. The gelling together of a couple is not automatic. It requires work, and counseling helps this to be easier and gives pointers of where to focus more work from couple to couple.

So, I say, be wise - go for counseling. Do not wait to get into trouble first. If your spouse needs persuasion first – go ahead and persuade them to go for counseling. You will rejoice when you see the results. Do not despise counseling!

Remember the word of God says in Psalms 24 vs 3, *"By wisdom a house is built and by understanding it is established."*

True wisdom and understanding comes through counseling, so, have a counselor for your marriage.

#RelationshipWise

#CounselingWorks

CHAPTER 22

CONFLICT RESOLUTION

> *"If it is possible, as much as it depends on you, live peaceably with all men,"* Romans 12vs18.

The above scripture teaches us to live peaceably with all men...and that includes spouses. In fact – especially spouses, for charity begins at home. Now, we all know that no matter how much a couple loves one another, there is always going to be a time when they will disagree. Love for each other is not immunity to disagreement. Let no one lie to you, each couple will have a type of conflict between them one way or the other, and at one point or another. These may be caused by the couple's own misunderstanding between the two of them, or they can be caused by the influence of friends, relatives, workmates, or other aspects of life. Whatever the reason, there are going to be conflicts here and there in every relationship.

It is therefore important to know how to resolve conflicts as a couple. Every couple must be trained to resolve its own conflicts amicably – without violence. No matter the source of conflict, a wise (trained) couple must resolve it comfortably – that is – without violence whether verbal or physical.

Clinical psychologist Russell Grieger in 2015 suggested that disagreements have four possible outcomes:

1. The outcome is good for the first person but not the second.
   It is a win-lose situation, and it is undesirable. One person gets what they want, while the other is left defeated, possibly feeling hurt, angry, and resentful. Such feelings can end up resurfacing into other areas of the relationship.
2. The outcome benefits the second person but not the first.
   This is another win-lose scenario like above. Only that it is the second person who is left feeling defeated, thwarted, and slighted.
3. The outcome is bad for both people.
   The third option is bad for both people in the relationship. It is a lose-lose situation and is usually a result of stubbornness on both sides when each thinks it is better for both to lose rather than allow the other to win – so neither gives in.
4. A resolution if found that is appropriate for both people.
   This is when the partners work on an equally beneficial outcome and achieve a win-win situation. Neither person is feeling thwarted or defeated leading to increased confidence and trust in the relationship. This option is the healthiest for the

long-term and avoids the downward spiral in the relationship.

How to resolve relationship conflicts in 4 steps

Step1 – Eliminate relations disturbances.
The first thing to do is to remove or to reduce emotions that will get in the way of conflict resolution. These things are hurt, anger and resentment. Without getting rid of these, neither side is going to listen patiently and openly to what the other is saying.

Step 2 – Commit to a win-win resolution.
Each party must find a solution that works for both equally. The couple must remain motivated and open to change.

Step 3 – Adopt purposeful listening.
This is called "active listening" in counseling, and it is vital. A win-win solution is possible when both parties listen to each other intently, purposefully avoiding judgement and censorship. When both get to really understanding each other, a win-win solution is possible.

Step 4 – Practise synergistic brainstorming
A couple will progress by having removed any emotional contamination adopted to a win-win mindset and fully committed to a win for both parties. The couple can share ideas, hopes, needs, goals, and concerns until finding a solution that satisfies both.

It may be important to note that a partly win-win situation does not mean each getting 100% of what they want – but a workable compromise for both may be the best the situation can allow in some cases.

So, when all is said and done, it is important to note that any couple willing and determined to resolve their conflicts amicably, can do so and attain win-win resolution when they follow through this practice.

#ConflictsAreResolved

CHAPTER

23

RENEW AND REFRESH YOUR MARRIAGE

Any marriage can easily become a drudge and boring if the couple does not spice it up. Routines and schedules in life are unavoidable but we must create moments of spontaneous fun and even planned fun. We cannot avoid going to work, doing school runs, shopping, parent-teacher meetings, church and work-related meetings and trips out of town. If we are not careful, all this can consume us to the point that a couple can end up being housemates, joint childminders, bill co-payers and nothing more. This must be avoided.

A marriage must remain exciting, romantic, and not always predictable. It can be hard to maintain a fun-filled relationship, but every couple must strive for it. Some couples get old before they are old! Kids are hard work but also a blessing and we must be able to work around them. Not every shift at work has our names on it – even the high paying weekend and public holiday shifts. Not every church leadership meeting can be attended – especially at the risk of marriage. In other words, attend the church meetings as much as you can but not on your anniversary, your spouse's birthday etc. It is good to communicate with your pastor and your other leaders that you are unavailable because you must attend to something important.

So, what exactly can one do to avoid his marriage going stale? Here are some strong recommendations and suggestions:

1. Arrange date nights – Call in a childminder, or as a community, take turns to look after children so that other couples can go for date nights. You go for dinner, probably a movie, bonding or go watch live sports together.
2. Never forget important dates – Anniversaries, birthdays and other important dates must be celebrated.
3. Play games at home – Just the two of you can play a game or two while the children are away or asleep, checkers, chess, scrabble and so on.
4. Be spontaneous – Sneak out – the two of you for an ice-cream or a coffee round the corner. Also have spontaneous sex when the situation allows – in the shower and everywhere else when there is adequate privacy. Who ever said sex is for the bedroom only?
5. Dance – I usually surprise my wife by playing a love song and hold her and dance even with our children around. They happen to be adults now but even when they are young in your case, it is not a problem. To some extent they must see their parents exhibiting love towards each other so that they get a positive attitude towards marriage.
6. Watch good shows together – Clean comedy and detective series are my favorites. Laugh together. You can also watch sports together on TV. I remember in the early days of our marriage during the 1990 Soccer World Cup – my wife made

it a point to playfully annoy me by joining with my cousin in supporting Argentina because she liked Diego Maradona. I wanted her to support Brazil – the real football artists. Well, I had the last laugh! Brazil soundly thrashed Maradona and the Argentines and my cousin left my house sulking with me teasing him. And as for Gwen – no problem... it was just a game! We still talk about that day up to now and we laugh about it.
7. Surprise each other – Husbands must learn to bring home some goodies as surprises for their wives – flowers, chocolates, lingerie, and other things you know she loves. Wives can also surprise their husbands by cooking that special favorite meal of his while he least expects it. Buy him that fancy tie he commented on when brother John wore his to church.

There are other things a couple can do to avoid drudgery in marriage. It requires sacrifice, it requires energy – but with the right mindset, anything and everything is possible. Never allow your marriage to get rusty and never take each other for granted. No one will ever come and re-ignite the fire in your marriage and your romance. You must do it yourself.

So, what are you waiting for? Do something fun and special TODAY!

#Don'tGrowOldBeforeYou'reOld

CHAPTER 24

MESSAGE TO THE VETERANS

> *"The older woman likewise... that they admonish the young women to love their husbands, to love their children ... chaste, homemakers, good, obedient to their own husbands..."*
> Titus 2 vs 3-5.

> *"Likewise, exhort young men to be sober minded...showing integrity, reverence..."* Titus 2 vs 6-7.

Paul wrote to Titus to encourage older women to exhort younger women to be good to their families; and older men are asked to exhort young men to be sober minded and be of integrity. This call is for all of us "war vets" because we have fought the devil in the area of marriage and have won. The war, which I described in the introduction, was not easy – but God was always on our side.

It is important for us to teach the younger generation the sanctity of marriage, the sacredness of the vows we made, and that the marriage bed is to be kept undefiled. If God has graced you with a long marriage, impact someone, encourage someone. You are a hero! The devil fought you, but you and your spouse are still standing. Impart that to the young ones and give back to society. Do the work of God. Take a few couples under your wing and groom them and mentor them. Most people learn by seeing, so let the young couples see how you do it – how you relate.

So, I am calling upon all seniors – let us teach the emerging generation how marriage is done. Yes, styles of doing things and love names they call each other may change, but the fundamentals do not change, and it is those fundamentals that we must teach them. Let us teach the young men that it is never acceptable to beat the wife or scream at her. Mature ladies, please teach the young wives that honor, respect, and submission to their husbands is not a favor to your man but God's commandment.

'Oldies', let us shout from the mountain tops that heterosexual marriage, and only heterosexual marriage is of God – and let us be kept pure and be a blessing as God intends it to be – a picture of Christ and His church.

I am sure God will add to you more years to affect the younger generation as you start seriously giving back to society.
God bless you veterans! You have fought a good fight of faith.

Younger generation, let no devil lie to you or trick you – you are meant to enjoy and not endure your marriage. Remember marriage is the closest you can "experience" to heaven or hell on earth! Which one do you want to feel?

May God bless your marriage in all areas – all areas indeed!

#MyMarriageHeavenOrHellOnEarth

CONCLUSION

God surely made marriage to be enjoyed and not endured. He blessed the institution of marriage and has always desired that it reflects the relationship between Him and His church. He has blessed and equipped each couple with tools to cultivate their marriage and defend it. However, it depends upon each couple to make an effort and cultivate their marriage. As each couple decides to take a stand against the devil, the destroyer of marriages, God brings in abundant grace to make each couple win this battle. This battle is rigged in our favor. We can all enjoy our marriages and make them a little heaven on earth! I hope this book has given you motivation, hints, direction, and determination to fight for your marriage and make your marriage heaven on earth.

DR. TADIUS MAWOKO

Books by Drs. Tadius and Gwen Mawoko

- **Cross-Cultural Mission Work and Church Planting: Memoirs of a Young- Missionary Couple** by Dr. Tadius Mawoko.
- **Towards Marital Bliss – 21-day Marriage Devotional for Women** by Dr. Gwen Mawoko.
- **Toward Marital Bliss: Marriage Nuggets** by Dr. Gwen Mawoko.

Future Books and Services

- **Teaching Moments with Dr. Tad** by Dr. Tadius Mawoko (Coming soon).
- **Before You say I Do: Premarital Counseling for those about to wed** by Drs. Tadius and Gwen Mawoko (Coming soon).

Author contact information

Email: tad@tadandgwen.com
Website: www.tadandgwen.com
Facebook: Pastor Tadius Mawoko

DR. TADIUS MAWOKO

Milton Keynes UK
Ingram Content Group UK Ltd.
UKHW020011151124
451207UK00018B/234